Vocabulary Lists and Activities

for the PreK–2 Classroom

Vocabulary Lists and Activities for the PreK–2 Classroom

Susan E. Israel

Integrating Vocabulary, Children's Literature, and Think-Alouds to Enhance Literacy

For information:

Corwin Press
A SAGE Company
2455 Teller Road
Thousand Oaks, California 91320
www.corwinpress.com

SAGE India Pvt. Ltd.
B 1/I 1 Mohan Cooperative Industrial Area
Mathura Road, New Delhi
India 110 044

SAGE Ltd.
1 Oliver's Yard
55 City Road
London EC1Y 1SP
United Kingdom

SAGE Asia-Pacific Pte. Ltd.
33 Pekin Street #02-01
Far East Square
Singapore 048763

Printed in the United States of America.

Library of Congress Cataloging-in-Publication Data

Israel, Susan E.
Vocabulary lists and activities for the preK–2 classroom : integrating vocabulary, children's literature, and think-alouds to enhance literacy/Susan E. Israel.
p. cm.
Includes bibliographical references and index.
ISBN 978-1-4129-5350-4 (cloth)
ISBN 978-1-4129-5351-1 (pbk.)
1. Vocabulary—Study and teaching (Early childhood)—Activity programs. 2. English language—Composition and exercises—Study and teaching (Early childhood) 3. Language arts (Early childhood) I. Title.

LB1139.5.L35I87 2009
372.6′1—dc22 2008011276

This book is printed on acid-free paper.

08 09 10 11 12 10 9 8 7 6 5 4 3 2 1

Acquisitions Editor: Cathy Hernandez
Editorial Assistant: Ena Rosen
Production Editor: Cassandra Margaret Seibel
Copy Editor: Alison Hope
Typesetter: C&M Digitals (P) Ltd.
Proofreader: Scott Oney
Indexer: Terri Corry
Cover Designer: Monique Hahn

Contents

Preface

At the 2005 National Reading Conference in Miami, Florida, where the research on primary word usage that informs this book was presented, one of the discussants, Michael Pressley, a distinguished professor from Michigan State University and the leading expert in the field of comprehension and literacy, stated that comprehension and vocabulary were underdeveloped areas. During the symposium discussion, there was a lot of emphasis placed on teaching students, especially primary grade students, words—many words. This book attempts to respond to this needs-based discussion. The vocabulary research that inspired this book was conducted by Dr. Edward B. Fry and me. Dr. Fry is professor emeritus of education at Rutgers University and is known for his *Fry List of High-Frequency Words* and the *Fry Readability Formula.* His spirit and wisdom guided our collaborative research effort that produced the word lists for this book.

HOW THIS BOOK IS ORGANIZED

I have organized this book into three main parts, based on the way reading and writing are currently taught in primary grade classrooms, and motivated by the No Child Left Behind, Reading First, and Early Reading First initiatives.

Part I focuses on using oral language to develop vocabulary. The word lists in this section are integrated with word learning experiences that occur during oral language. Research-based literacy strategies in this part focus on engaging students in conversation and dialogic strategies with children's literature.

Part II features word lists that focus on developing vocabulary through storybook read-alouds. These lists are integrated with children's literature and include research-based activities specifically designed to develop vocabulary during read-aloud experiences.

Part III is about the development of vocabulary through writing. Writing provides opportunities for students to use familiar words and learn new words, and it promotes reading comprehension and reading success.

Within each of the three parts, you will find the chapters. Each chapter begins with an overview of the thematic topic and the type of vocabulary words that can be found within the chapter. A wide range of strategies and several word lists that connect to the topic and that are designed to enhance the overall word learning process make up the remainder of each chapter. The lists include the words from the Israel and Fry (2005) research on primary grade students' word usage in their writing. These words are presented in **bold** type for easy identification. Additional words are included to elaborate on the topic, build vocabulary, and make connections with words in meaningful contexts through children's literature selections. Each chapter also offers literacy integrations for reading and writing in the classroom, writing prompts to integrate with journal activities, children's literature read-aloud suggestions, think-aloud suggestions to enhance vocabulary, or suggestions for parent involvement or home–school connections.

The chapter themes are as follows:

Part I: Vocabulary Voices I Hear

Chapter 1: Words that build school success

Chapter 2: Words that enhance the alphabetic principle

Chapter 3: Phonics and teamwork

Part II: Read-to-Me Words

Chapter 4: Words that provide extensions in new genres

Chapter 5: Words that build nonfiction vocabulary

Chapter 6: Words that highlight cultural celebrations

Part III: How I Use Words I Can Read

Chapter 7: Words that define a writer's craft

How the Lists Were Designed

We compiled the word lists from original writing samples from students in Grades K–3. We asked teachers to submit original writing samples: the teacher had not edited the writings, and the teacher had not asked the student to revise the writings. We counted the words in each sample, and organized them based on frequency of use. As of this writing, there is no substantive volume prepared specifically for primary grade teachers that is devoted to guiding teachers to develop their students' vocabulary in an organized manner. In addition to filling a gap in the field of vocabulary reading and writing instruction, this book serves a second purpose: to document the most recent research-based writing words, organized around practical themes on topics specifically chosen for students in PreK to Grade 3.

I recommend that the reader approach this book by first reviewing the table of contents to understand how the material is organized. Next, I suggest paging through the book and sampling various themes of interest. Since I like highlighting text that is important to me, I suggest the reader then return to the table of contents to highlight themes of particular interest. Finally, I suggest the reader share lists from this book with students and their parents, and challenge them to choose a few word lists they would like to learn at home or in school.

WHO WILL FIND THIS BOOK USEFUL?

The main audience for this book is teachers of students in kindergarten through Grade 2, although educators at all grade levels may find it useful. Following is a summary of how literacy educators can use this book:

- Individual classroom teachers who want to develop increased levels of vocabulary acquisition throughout the school year can use this work as a source of vocabulary words, activities, and writing ideas developed around classroom and school themes such as community.
- Teachers who work with English language learners will find the themes useful. Themes lists start with vocabulary related to the natural environment, and then move on to oral environments, trade books, and then higher-quality literature, which leads to vocabulary gains.
- Grade-level groups of teachers can use this book as a tool for planning effective literacy instruction based on recommendations on vocabulary development from the *Report of the National Reading Panel* (National Institute of Child Health and Human Development [NICHD], 2000).
- Literacy coaches and reading specialists can use this book to develop vocabulary instruction with primary grade teachers.
- Reading specialists who work with intermediate-level readers might benefit from words based on authentic writing samples.
- Intermediate-grade teachers who want to bridge the gaps in vocabulary might find it useful.
- Librarians who design theme-based library activities using children's literature to increase vocabulary and reading might benefit.
- Districts attempting to build a common vocabulary and consistency in vocabulary instruction while curriculum is aligned with goals and state standards can use this book.
- Professors of early childhood, elementary, or literacy education can use this book as a primary text in word study programs or as a supplementary text to demonstrate research-based word learning strategies with students.
- Study groups or professional development in-service programs can use the table of contents as a guide to focus on specific areas that need to be developed within the school literacy framework.
- Parents and caregivers who want to fuel vocabulary development in the home environment will value the recommendations of children's literature and the suggested word learning strategies.

HOW THIS BOOK WILL BENEFIT EDUCATORS AND THEIR STUDENTS

- This book will allow teachers to introduce a variety of words with ideas for using them in writing and language to their students.
- This book will allow teachers to move easily into a writing prompt, oral language development, and other dialogue for increasing and understanding the use of words.

- This book presents teachers with a guide to follow when integrating vocabulary words in speaking and writing.
- Each chapter of this book builds on the themes and word lists from the previous chapter to allow for continuous growth of learning for students.
- Beginning teachers can easily implement ideas, yet the book offers more experienced teachers with new and innovative methods.
- Each chapter offers literature connections and extensions, activities, think-alouds, and additional resources to support the teacher in the classroom.
- Technology links are provided for teachers to enhance their repertoire of vocabulary ideas.

The overarching benefit of this book and these word lists and strategies is to improve preschool and primary grade students' vocabulary so that their reading and writing skills will improve.

Acknowledgments

Corwin Press gratefully acknowledges the contributions of the following individuals:

Anita Barnes, Literacy and Math Specialist
Second Street School, Frankfort, KY

Gustava Cooper-Baker, Principal
Sanford B. Ladd Elementary School, Kansas City, MO

Jaimie Kalinowski, Teacher
Riley Elementary School, Arlington Heights, IL

Shannan McNair, Associate Professor of Human Development and Child Studies
Oakland University, Rochester, MI

Stephen Shepperd, Principal
Sunnyside Elementary School, Kellogg, ID

About the Author

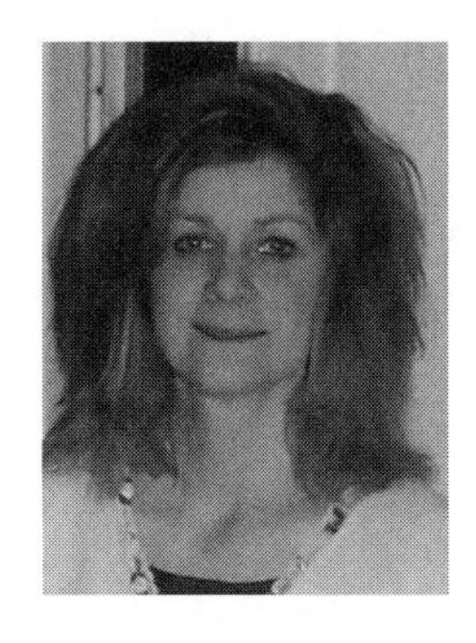

Susan E. Israel, PhD, is a literacy consultant in preschool literacy materials with Burkhart Network in Indianapolis, Indiana. Her research agenda focuses on reading comprehension that pertains to all aspects of literacy, such as vocabulary development, writing, and metacognition. She is a member of the National Reading Conference and the International Reading Association. She served as the president of the History of Reading, Special Interest Group in 2006–2007. She was awarded the 2005 Panhellenic Council Outstanding Professor Award at the University of Dayton. She was the 1998 recipient of the teacher-researcher grant from the International Reading Association, where she has served and been a member for more than a decade. She is author or editor of several books, including *Metacognition in Literacy Learning* (2005), *Reading First and Beyond* (2005), *Collaborative Literacy: Engaging Gifted Strategies for All Learners* (2006), *Poetic Possibilities: Poems to Enhance Literacy Learning* (2006), *Quotes to Inspire Great Reading Teachers* (2006), *Comprehensive Guide to Teacher Research* (2007), *Dynamic Literacy Instruction* (2007), *The Ethical Educator* (2007), *Metacognitive Assessments* (2007), *Shaping the Reading Field* (2007), and *Handbook of Research on Reading Comprehension* (2008).

This book is a result of Dr. Israel's research conducted on a national level and presented with Dr. Edward B. Fry at the 2005 National Reading Conference in Miami, Florida.

About the Guest Contributor

T. Lee Williams is an assistant professor of reading education in the Department of Curriculum and Teaching at Auburn University in Auburn, Alabama. She spent nine years as an elementary teacher in urban, rural, and suburban schools. Her research interests include integrated literacy strategies and the characteristics of effective teachers.

Introduction

VOCABULARY WORDS FOR PRIMARY GRADE STUDENTS

> *Vocabulary instruction that inspires such fascination needs to be robust: vigorous, strong, and powerful in effect. It also needs to be interactive and motivating.*
>
> ~Beck, McKeown, & Kucan (2002, p. x)

Vocabulary is a tool to communicate known words with others (Harris & Hodges, 1995). A first grader, who wrote the story about the alien in Figure 0.1, uses descriptive vocabulary to communicate information about the alien, which the student "does not love."

What captured my attention about this story was the way the young author explains his feeling about the alien in the first sentence. We know right away that the author does not love aliens. When children begin to have internal command of vocabulary, they begin to express thoughts and feelings confidently. Children

Figure 0.1

acquire or internalize words from the natural environment building from this repertoire of words to expand vocabulary through experiences with oral and written language. The vocabulary lists in this book are based on primary grade students' authentic writing samples. They are referred to as *authentic* because the teachers did not revise the writing samples, and they do not use writing prompts or require that the student fill in blanks. Which words in the lists are from the study? Which ones are added to supplement and extend the learning? The words from the study are presented in **bold** type. Additional words have been provided to supplement and extend the learning. Where appropriate, activities that include the use of high-quality children's books have been presented. The complete list of words from the study can be found in Chapter 7, List #38.

USING THESE LISTS TO DEVELOP VOCABULARY

Primary grade teachers who wish to develop children's vocabulary with the goal of improving reading instruction can use this book with integrated thematic units. Lists are organized around the everyday experiences of how children learn vocabulary:

- Through daily oral language engagements in the classroom, in social settings, and in the home environment
- By listening to adults read to them through storybooks and print-rich materials
- From independent reading using different types of literature, texts, and interactive reading tools

Educators will find the chapter topic themes valuable when planning curriculum for the school year or for quick lessons on theme-based word lists. The lists focus on needs of individual students. For example, with early primary grade children who are not yet reading, Part I will be valuable because the chapters focus on beginning word knowledge common to school literacy programs. Part II focuses on words they will encounter during read-aloud experiences. Part III presents words from text encounters using a variety of print-rich resources.

Teachers working in early childhood centers will benefit from the inclusion of strategically selected children's literature that supports each chapter's theme. Improving oral language development with early primary grade children is a goal in Early Reading First initiatives (Block & Israel, 2005). The book's research-based vocabulary activities are directly correlated with the children's literature and overarching part goals.

UNDERSTANDING EARLY READING FIRST AND READING FIRST VOCABULARY INSTRUCTIONAL GOALS

The following section defines vocabulary instructional goals of the Early Reading First and Reading First initiatives. Both initiatives are supported by findings from the *Report of the National Reading Panel* (NICHD, 2000). Vocabulary is essential to reading and reading comprehension. Increased vocabulary acquisition occurs indirectly or directly. Before children attend kindergarten, oral language experiences enhance overall word meanings learned. Children listen to adults before they are able to talk and communicate. Hearing vocabulary used in the context of conversations is the indirect beginning of vocabulary knowledge. Listening intently to adults during reading is another aspect of how children acquire vocabulary indirectly. As adults read to children, it is particularly effective when they stop and elaborate on new words or interesting words, discussing meaning in the context of the story. Once children are able to read independently, they learn more words as they encounter them. Unfamiliar words disrupt meaning construction; therefore, teaching children vocabulary strategies to use during independent reading is necessary. Direct instruction is another method to introduce word meaning and independent word building strategies.

Vocabulary instruction deepens when done effectively; it reinforces word learning. Specific strategies recommended through research from the National Reading Panel include the following:

- Introduce new words prior to reading.
- Teach students to use prior knowledge to make connections with new words.
- Provide extended instruction with repeated occurrences of vocabulary to help children learn new words.
- Teach new words in contexts that students encounter frequently.
- Use active engagement based on individual learning needs to promote word learning.
- Reinforce learning connections of new words by teaching specific words related to topics or organized around themes.
- Teach writing to help children understand more deeply the meaning of new words.
- Teach efficient use of vocabulary resources such as dictionaries, thesauruses, and glossaries to help students increase their knowledge of the meanings of words and to make connections with other words and multiple meanings.
- Teach the etymology, as well as affixes (prefixes and suffixes), and base words and root words to enhance vocabulary acquisition.

Choosing Words to Learn

Primary grade teachers should choose words carefully. There are three categories of words that can be taught: words particularly useful to the text, words that are very important to reading comprehension, and words that are difficult to read and understand. Often students find it difficult to decode words that have more than one meaning.

Many students will begin school with their own repertoire of vocabulary. One simple assessment that primary grade teachers can use with all the lists is to find out their students' level of word knowledge. For instance, teachers can invite students to generate lists of words they know. Teachers can establish levels of word knowledge and focus instructional time on learning related words, such as synonyms and antonyms or words that are more challenging. Word knowledge can be placed in the following levels:

- Unfamiliar words
- Somewhat familiar words
- Very familiar words

Based on the implications presented by Fry (2004), more common or higher frequency word correspondences should be taught first. Therefore, in this book initial chapters within each part build on words from the primary writing study that teachers should teach initially. As teachers begin to provide different literacy experiences, such as read-alouds, vocabulary knowledge builds if intentionally taught by the teacher.

SUMMARY

There are three primary goals of this book. The first goal is to integrate the findings based on an analysis of a national word study investigation of word utilization with primary grade children in the United States with natural word learning strategies. The second goal of this book is to communicate effective methods of building word skills through oral language, storybook reading, and independent reading. The third goal of this book is to utilize high-quality literature to help teachers of primary grade children integrate new vocabulary during the normal course of the day.

Exemplary literacy teachers use rich literacy materials during daily read-alouds and use these experiences as a way to motivate and engage students in literacy learning (Block, Oakar, & Hurt, 2002; Block & Mangieri, 2003). According to the *Report of the National Reading Panel* (NICHD, 2000), greater emphasis needs to be placed on vocabulary development. As Beck, McKeown, and Kucan (2002) stated in the beginning quote of this chapter, "Vocabulary instruction that inspires such fascination needs to be robust: vigorous, strong, and powerful in effect. It also needs to be interactive and motivating." Educators concerned with building primary grade children's vocabulary will find that the word lists inspire and fascinate children. The research-based instructional strategies combined with high-quality literature are robust and will motivate children to learn words and be inspired along the way.

PART I

Vocabulary Voices I Hear

Development of Vocabulary Through Oral Language Literacy

One of the first ways children learn vocabulary is through oral language. Adults like to encourage students to use oral language by asking questions or explaining what is on their mind. Figure I.1 encourages oral language through questioning. There are many other methods to develop oral language. As stated in *Put Reading First: The Research Building Blocks for Teaching Children to Read,*

> Young children learn word meanings through conversations with other people, especially adults. As they engage in these conversations, children often hear adults repeat words several times. They also may hear adults use new and interesting words. The more oral language experiences children have, the more word meanings they learn. (National Institute for Literacy, 2003, p. 35)

Part I includes lists of words that children typically hear during early oral language experiences. The words are the first level of words taught through oral language; oral language is the first method of instruction to help students acquire new vocabulary.

The vocabulary methods in Part I focus on using research-based oral language strategies and dialogic reading in small groups to increase vocabulary acquisition. Research-based strategies will assist teachers in helping children learn vocabulary through oral language. A new research-based strategy that has proven to be particularly effective with primary grade children is a method known as *dialogic reading.* Dialogic reading helps teachers structure their talk in ways that guide vocabulary development (McIntyre, Kyle, & Moore, 2006). Effective dialogic reading includes the following suggested teacher tips:

- Establish small groups of students.
- Sit students face-to-face.

Figure I.1

Our World . . . Let's Find Out About It

- What country looks like a boot?
- Find Portugal on the map.
- Is it warm or cold in the Antarctic?
- Is our planet round or square?
- If it is winter in Ireland, what season is it in Australia?
- In what country would you find a kangaroo?
- On what continents would you find lions and tigers?
- Find the island of Madagascar.
- Where does the Pope live?
- Find Iraq on the map.
- Find the largest city in Iraq.
- Name six kinds of fish that live in the ocean.

- Invite children to visualize the conversation they will have to help them think about what they will say so they can participate more effectively.
- Encourage discussion and spontaneous remarks.
- Allow children to respond to one another.
- Guide the discussion by demonstrating, explaining, and defining.
- Intervene when necessary to help students maintain effective discussions.

The vocabulary lists in this part are based on words that students encounter early in the primary grades. Teaching students words that they can use to be successful in school is important. In addition, words become meaningful to students because they are encountered in oral language experiences in school and at home.

Primary Grade Teachers' Resource Toolbox: Vocabulary Instructional Resources, Theory to Practice

Teaching Vocabulary

Blachowicz, C., & Fisher, P. (2002). *Teaching Vocabulary in All Classrooms* (2nd ed.). Columbus, OH: Merrill Prentice Hall. A valuable resource for teachers who want to increase knowledge of vocabulary instruction using research-based strategies. This book can also be indispensable for those who teach reading methods courses.

Tiered Vocabulary

Beck, I. A., McKeown, M. G., & Kucan, L. (2002). *Bringing Words to Life: Robust Vocabulary Instruction.* New York: Guilford Press. Learn how to organize vocabulary words based on three tiers of word knowledge. This book will benefit primary teachers who want a method on how to differentiate instruction through word lists.

Vygotskian Speaking

Vygotsky, L. (2000, rev. ed.). *Thought and Language.* Cambridge: MIT Press. Oral language development and dialogue was the framework for the theory of "zo-ped," a term used by the author to explain his theories of the zone of proximal development. This theory-based book provides the context for many of the social experiences of children where rich oral language is developed.

1

School Success

Life is tons of discipline. Your first discipline is your vocabulary; then your grammar and your punctuation. Then, in your exuberance and bounding energy you say you're going to add to that. Then you add rhyme and meter. And your delight is in that power.

~Robert Frost

THEME REFLECTION

When students enter school for the first time, they are so excited to learn new things. They are proud of simple things that older children and even adults take for granted. When my youngest daughter was in kindergarten, she really liked to tell stories, and she could hardly wait for "show-and-tell" day. She would plan her show-and-tell items weeks in advance and have them laid out in the order that she wanted to take them to school. If I asked her why she wanted to take those items to school, she would be able to tell me the rationale for each. I thought this was wonderful and I loved hearing her stories. As an educator, I think about the value of oral language and vocabulary development. This chapter focuses on themes related to school success. Knowing words about concepts related to school would help students' vocabulary increase tremendously. In addition, the "school" words are most likely the children's first encounters with school vocabulary. Use the words in this theme to help build oral language vocabulary, as well as confidence about school. To paraphrase Robert Frost, I reflect on how a child's delight is in the power of words.

LIST #1 BACK TO SCHOOL

Teachers look forward to going back to school because they get to start anew. Children love to buy new school supplies and new clothes as they prepare for their very first day. Going to school is a big deal for children, especially primary grade children, because the classrooms are exciting and they love to learn new things. The words on this list are some that children will encounter when they go to school for the first time, as well as the words they might need to relearn at the start of a new school year.

activity
alphabet
assignment
bell
book
bulletin
bus
busy
center
chair
classroom
coach
crayon
desk
drawing
flag
fountain
friend
games
grade
homework
learn
liberty
marker
neighbor
newsletter
paper
parent
pencil
people
practice
principal
prize
read
recess
reward
rule
school
signature
sticker
story
student
substitute
table
teacher
toys
workbook
write
year

Journal Writing Prompts

My name is ___ and I like to . . .

My favorite . . .

We went to school and when we arrived our teacher gave us . . .

Vocabulary Literacy Scaffolds: In order for students to be successful in school, they need to understand the world around them. Words that teachers will be using every day throughout the school year should be words students recognize and with which they are familiar. Use the words in this list to send home with parents on the first day of school and invite parents to read the list together so their primary grade child can become familiar with the language of school.

CHILDREN'S LITERATURE SELECTION

Book: Brennan-Nelson, D. (2004). *My Teacher Likes to Say.* New York: Sleeping Bear Press.

Theme Integration: The focus of this book is on expressions children might hear when they go to school, such as "Put on your thinking cap." The book uses funny and confusing expressions that provide some of life's most valuable lessons.

Literature Vocabulary Extensions:

behavior
cliché
encourage
expression
homework
hungry
idiom
imagine
powerful
proud
proverb
response
special

Sample Vocabulary Development Think-Aloud:

Teacher Would Read:	*Teacher Might Stop and Say:*
"Does your teacher ever say things that you think are quite amusing?" "Does your teacher ever say things that you find a bit confusing?"	Isn't that interesting: the words "amusing" and "confusing" rhyme. I know what amusing means and that is something funny. I am not sure what confusing means or what this person is implying. I think it might mean mixing something up or not understanding. Let me read further.
"My teacher says some funny things like, 'The squeaky wheel gets the oil,' 'Don't beat around the bush,' and 'A watched pot never boils.'"	Oh, now I think I know what the word "confusing" means. It means mixing up something with something else. Sometimes confusing sayings like the one we just heard are called idioms, proverbs, or clichés.

Oral Language Development: When you reach the middle of the book, stop and invite children to share funny expressions they have heard their teacher say. Students share with the group and explain their favorites and what they mean to them. Reinforce vocabulary by using these new words.

LIST #2 PEOPLE I KNOW

Primary grade children like to read and write about people they know. They especially like to write about their family members and their friends. Names are very important to them, so it is important to make sure students know names of their family and friends, as well as titles. This list contains descriptors or titles of people who are important to primary grade children.

aunt
baby
babysitter
boy
brother
bus driver
class
coach
cook
cousins
dad
daddy
doctor
family
father
friends
girl
grandfather
grandma
grandmother
grandpa
mom
mommy
mother
nurse
people
person
police officer
sister
teacher
team
uncle

Journal Writing Prompts

When I grow up, I want to be a . . .

When we went to the ___ we saw a . . .

When our ___ went outside, a big . . .

Vocabulary Idea Share: Pass out a sheet of paper with the names of students in the classroom. Have students work in pairs or with an adult to write one nice thought after each person's name on the list. The teacher should also include his or her name. When the students are done, have them cut each of the names apart and pass out the sentence strip to the students in their classroom. This will help students get to know each other and build community in the classroom at the beginning of the school year. Use this idea with List #3, which summarizes kind phrases to use in the classroom when talking or writing about others (adapted from Howard, 2004).

CHILDREN'S LITERATURE SELECTION

Book: Lucas, D. (2003). *Halibut Jackson.* New York: Alfred A. Knopf.

Theme Integration: The title of this book prompts students to think about names, which is the theme of Word List #2.

Literature Vocabulary Extensions:

indoors
invitation
library
majesty
notice
park
RSVP
shame
shops
shy
suit

Sample Vocabulary Development Think-Aloud:

Teacher Would Read:	*Teacher Might Stop and Say:*
"The title of this book is *Halibut Jackson.*"	Do you think Halibut Jackson is a funny name? I do not know anyone who has the name of Halibut. Jackson sounds like a first name to me. Who in here has heard of someone with the name of Halibut? I wonder if people notice Halibut because of his name?
"Halibut Jackson was shy."	When I was a little girl, my parents said I was very shy. They said I did not talk much. Shy is a word to describe someone. Do you think you are shy? What does shy mean to you? Let's find out why Halibut is shy.

Oral Language Development: This is a fun book to help students become familiar with classmates. Have students say their first and last name and one word that might describe them.

LIST #3 KINDNESS COUNTS

At the beginning of the school year, help the children in your classroom understand what type of language you expect to hear or not hear from them. This list contains positive words and synonyms that promote a positive attitude and kindness toward others. This list can be given to students or displayed in your classroom.

dear—beloved, precious, valued

excited—eager, energized, thrilled

favorite—preferred, ideal, ultimate

friend—ally, companion, pal

great—awesome, grand, splendid

happy—content, pleased, joyful

help—assist, facilitate, lend

hope—anticipate, trust, wish

kind—charitable, generous, giving

kindness—consideration, humanity, sympathy

likes—enjoys, relishes, cherishes

love—adore, admire, respect

nice—**kind**, considerate, polite

please—**give,** delight, satisfy

pretty—beautiful, **cute,** gorgeous

sincerely—respectfully, warmly, gratefully

sweet—caring, **kind,** considerate

thank—appreciate, be grateful for, value

together—collectively, jointly, mutually

turn—alternate, exchange, rotate

yes—agreed, okay, sure

Journal Writing Prompts

My friend and I . . .

We became excited when . . .

After working together on the ____, we . . .

Vocabulary Idea Share: Another community-building activity for the start of the school year is to make compliment posters. Have students print their names on a sheet of construction paper. Invite them to decorate their names. Once everyone is done, begin passing the name posters around the room and have each child write one compliment on each paper. Younger children could use stickers that have kind words on them. Hang the posters in the room for the parents to see at back-to-school night.

CHILDREN'S LITERATURE SELECTION

Book: Reynolds, P. H. (2004). *Ish.* New York: Candlewick Press.

Theme Integration: This book emphasizes being kind to others. A sibling displays an act of kindness that is somewhat unexpected.

Literature Vocabulary Extensions:

burst
crumpled
drawing
energized
exclaimed
favorite
gallery
ish
journal
laughter
sneered

Sample Vocabulary Development Think-Aloud:

Teacher Would Read:	*Teacher Might Stop and Say:*
"One day, Ramon was drawing a vase of flowers. His brother, Leon, leaned over his shoulder. Leon burst out laughing."	"Bursts" is a word I am familiar with. Have you ever seen a balloon pop? That is what I think of when I read the word "burst." In this sentence, it means that Leon suddenly started laughing, or that he started to laugh unexpectedly. Yesterday, when (name a student in the class) told me a funny joke, I burst out laughing. I did this in a nice way but I think maybe that Leon is laughing to be mean. Why do you think he burst out laughing?

Oral Language Development: "Ish" is a funny word. Discuss the meaning with your students. After reading this story, have students use the word list above to create a new story about a character in the book or several students in the class. Share the story with the class and make sure that the story uses the funny word "ish."

LIST #4 MY FAVORITES

Children love to talk and write about their favorite things. When teachers give students the opportunity to share their favorite food, activities, people, and places, they get to know the students better. Students will enjoy being able to talk and write about some of their favorites using this list as a resource. This list can also be used as a writing prompt to generate word lists about students' favorite things.

Foods	*Activities*	*People*	*Places*
apples	doing art	coach	city
bananas	playing **basketball**	**dad**	**farm**
cake	**cooking**	doctor	**home**
candy	drawing	**friend**	**house**
cookies	**eating**	**grandma**	**mall**
corn	playing **football**	**grandpa**	**movie**
fruit	playing **games**	**mom**	**outside**
hamburger	going on a **hayride**	nurse	**park**
hot dog	playing **hockey**	police officer	**pool**
ice cream	painting	**Santa**	**room**
juice	going to a **party**	teacher	**school**
pizza	reading		**shop**
potatoes	playing in the **snow**		**store**
stuffing	playing **soccer**		**zoo**
turkey	**swinging**		
	trick-or-treating		

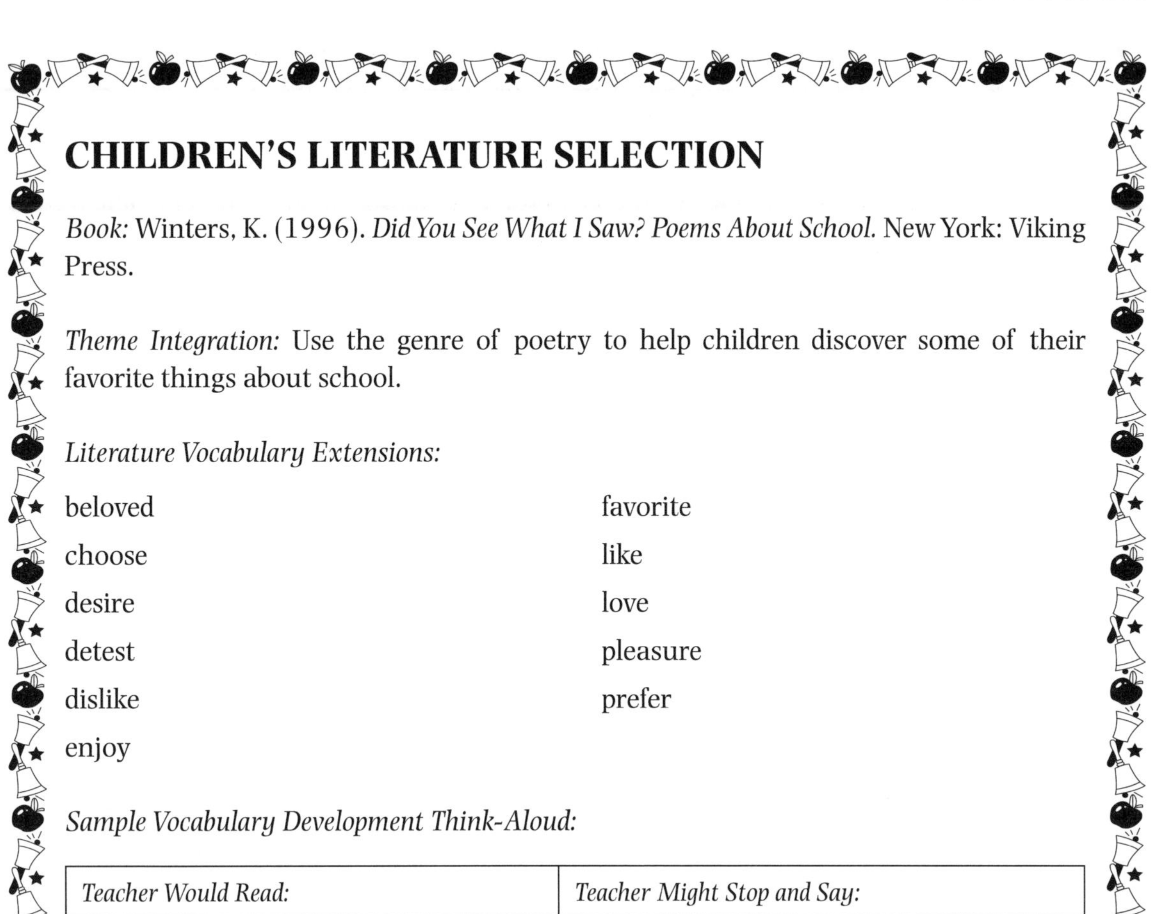

CHILDREN'S LITERATURE SELECTION

Book: Winters, K. (1996). *Did You See What I Saw? Poems About School.* New York: Viking Press.

Theme Integration: Use the genre of poetry to help children discover some of their favorite things about school.

Literature Vocabulary Extensions:

beloved
choose
desire
detest
dislike
enjoy
favorite
like
love
pleasure
prefer

Sample Vocabulary Development Think-Aloud:

Teacher Would Read:	*Teacher Might Stop and Say:*
"Blizzard. No school! A snow day! Bet the teacher's really mad! Today's the day we would have had our math test. Too bad! How sad! I'm glad! Whoopee!"	A blizzard is a very bad snowstorm that usually impairs vision. When I was little we had a very bad blizzard and school was closed for two weeks. When I was home, I preferred to go outside and play in the snow. I also enjoyed making snow forts.

Oral Language Development: Using different ways to say "favorite," have children tell what they would do on a snow day. Have them explain why they pick each activity.

LIST #5 CLASSROOM JOBS

Building community is important, especially at the start of the school year. Giving each student in the class a job gives them all the opportunity to take ownership of the classroom and to assume responsibilities. Use this list to determine job assignments on a rotating basis for each student in your class and to teach them new vocabulary words about each job. A title and fun description will help you have fun with classroom jobs and motivate students to get excited about helping out in the classroom.

Birthday Buddies—A group of students who make cards and decorate desks on birthdays

Bulletin Board Buddies—A group of students who decorate bulletin boards

Center Star—Organizes centers

Class Historian—Records daily events in a journal or book

Closet Keeper—Keeps the closet cleaned and organized

Compliment Caller—Gives compliments to students who need encouragement

Desk Dude—Organizes desks at the beginning or end of each day

Environmentalist—Makes sure the room and school areas are clean

Eraser Emperor—Responsible for cleaning erasers and organizing chalk or marker board

Gift Giver—Delivers materials to the students when things are brought to the classroom

Go Getter—Responsible for running errands in the school

Hallway Heroes—Responsible for decorating the hall with student papers

Homework Helpers—Writes down or checks posted homework assignments

Librarian Lover—Responsible for tracking books that are checked out

Line Leader—Is first in line and leads the students when going places

Mail Carrier—Passes out mail to students

Naturalist—Cares for plants and pets

Odd Job Officer—Does random jobs that need to be done daily or weekly

Paper Pal—Passes out papers

Pencil Pal—Responsible for making sure pencil sharpener is clean

Reading Rocker—Responsible for organizing books in the classroom

Recess Runner—Responsible for making sure everyone is included during recess

Shelf Shuffler—Keeps shelves organized

Special Stars—A group of students who do special jobs as they come up

Sticker Star—Places stickers on special achievement posters

Story Starter—Responsible for thinking of a story starter for journal writing assignments

Teacher's Angel—Watches over the teacher to make sure nothing has been forgotten

Time Keeper—Responsible for keeping time when necessary

Treat Team—Helps pass out treats on treat days

Window Watchers—Responsible for shutting windows at the end of the day

CHILDREN'S LITERATURE SELECTION

Book: Shaw, M. D. (2002). *Ten Amazing People and How They Changed the World.* New York: Skylight Paths Publishing.

Theme Integration: Students need to understand that they also have responsibilities in the classroom. This book is about amazing people who had challenging responsibilities to make the world a better place.

Literature Vocabulary Extensions:

advocate
charity
citizen
compassion
courage
homeless
independence
leader
moral
neighbor
persecution
social justice
worldly

Sample Vocabulary Development Think-Aloud:

Teacher Would Read:	*Teacher Might Stop and Say:*
"Dorothy Day was a young newspaper reporter in New York City when she began her lifelong mission of helping poor people and working for social change."	I have never been to New York City but I have always desired to go. I do know there are many homeless people who need a compassionate leader like Dorothy to advocate for social change. She helped the poor people in the city. What can we do to help poor people? Is it our job to do so?

Oral Language Development: Use the nonfiction book to learn about individual leaders of interest to your students. Use the words on the list to help them describe people they know who are amazing.

LIST #6 UNDERSTANDING DIRECTIONS

In the primary grades, students learn how to read and follow directions. Teachers can help their students be more successful at following directions by giving them a list of vocabulary words and helping them understand what they are to do for each direction given. Once students have a visual understanding of the directions, they will become more confident in the classroom.

ask
color
cut
draw
eat
glue
help
open
outside
paint
play
please
practice
read
take
write

Vocabulary Idea Share: Use a chart to help students become familiar with the type of direction they need to know. To help students make meaningful connections, help students draw a picture to help them remember the word for each direction. Use the list to prompt students to put the word in a complete sentence that gives specific directions.

CHILDREN'S LITERATURE SELECTION

Book: Herrera, J. F. (2000). *The Upside Down Boy.* New York: Children's Book Press.

Theme Integration: Using directions in our daily lives and in different cultures.

Literature Vocabulary Extensions:

campesinos
catching
city
conductor
harmonica
jumping
reading
recess
sombrero
steep
street
stuck
valley

Sample Vocabulary Development Think-Aloud:

Teacher Would Read:	*Teacher Might Stop and Say:*
"When I was little, my family spent years working in the fields as campesinos."	"Campesinos" must be a word to describe a person who lives in the village. I hear a word that tells me about the boy. If a boy is working in the fields, he might be picking corn or some other fruit or vegetable.

Oral Language Development: Have the students select a new word and draw a picture of that word. Students can use all the pictures together to tell a new story.

LIST #7 SCHOOL THEMES

At the beginning of the school year, teachers begin planning classroom themes for the year. This list of classroom themes focuses on building a community in the classroom rather than on specific things like bears, dogs, or dinosaurs.

acceptance
achievement
adventure
attentiveness
bravery
careers
caring
celebrations
character
charity
collaboration
community
companionship
courage
courtesy
creativity
determination
discipline
discovery
diversity
dreams
faith
family
forgiveness
fortitude
freedom
friendship
goals
government
gratitude
happiness
heroes
imagination
inquiry
kindness
knowledge
leadership
learning
love
merciful
neighbors
patience
peace
perseverance
pride
question
resilience
respect
responsibility
reverence
sacrifice
seasons
service
spirit
talent
teamwork
truth
understanding
united
unity
value
wisdom
worldly

Vocabulary Idea Share: Teachers can select words from this list to discuss with their students, as well as post the possible themes and ask them to pick a few of their favorites for the year. Students can add their own theme words to the list.

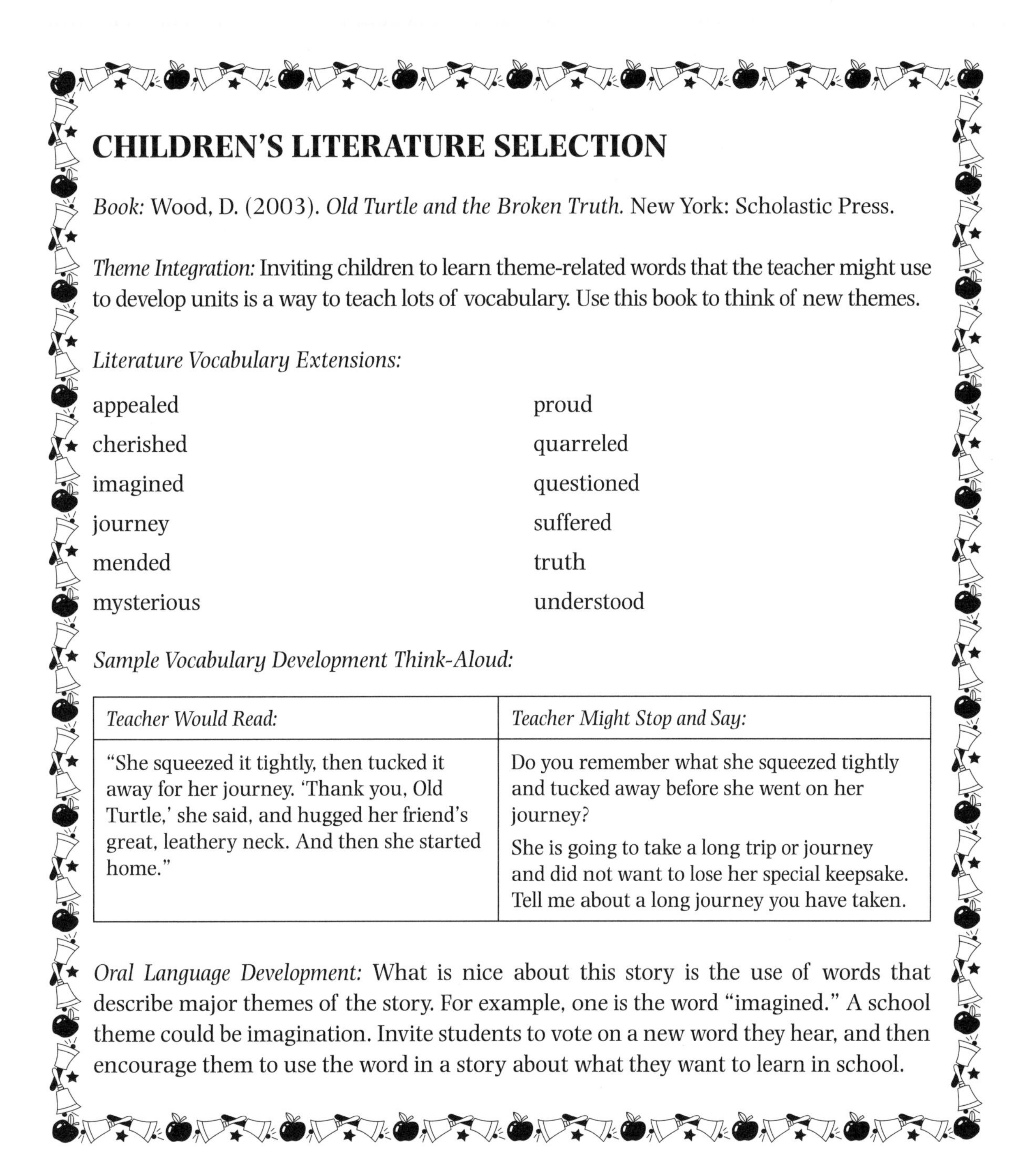

CHILDREN'S LITERATURE SELECTION

Book: Wood, D. (2003). *Old Turtle and the Broken Truth.* New York: Scholastic Press.

Theme Integration: Inviting children to learn theme-related words that the teacher might use to develop units is a way to teach lots of vocabulary. Use this book to think of new themes.

Literature Vocabulary Extensions:

appealed
cherished
imagined
journey
mended
mysterious
proud
quarreled
questioned
suffered
truth
understood

Sample Vocabulary Development Think-Aloud:

Teacher Would Read:	*Teacher Might Stop and Say:*
"She squeezed it tightly, then tucked it away for her journey. 'Thank you, Old Turtle,' she said, and hugged her friend's great, leathery neck. And then she started home."	Do you remember what she squeezed tightly and tucked away before she went on her journey? She is going to take a long trip or journey and did not want to lose her special keepsake. Tell me about a long journey you have taken.

Oral Language Development: What is nice about this story is the use of words that describe major themes of the story. For example, one is the word "imagined." A school theme could be imagination. Invite students to vote on a new word they hear, and then encourage them to use the word in a story about what they want to learn in school.

LIST #8 PARENT VOLUNTEERS

Teachers need help from parents. and parents love to help. Presented below are ideas for how to use parent volunteers in your classroom. Students can learn words that pertain to how parents can help in the classroom.

cutout activities
decorate classroom during holidays
deliver or pick up things in the community
develop film
do odd jobs
eat lunch with students
evaluate Web sites or books
gather library books
gather museum items
grade papers
help at recess
help at social events
Internet research
laminate
lead small-group activities
make books
make learning centers
make phone calls
mentor students
organize book clubs
photocopy papers
plan field trips
plan parent workshops
plan special events
prepare activities
prepare bulletin boards
prepare newsletters
prepare phone tree
prepare treats
research topics
send mail
set up displays
special events
supervise students during movies
take photographs
wash desks
write grant proposals
write letters

Tips on Getting Volunteers

1. Post jobs at back-to-school night and invite parents to sign up.
2. Include a special sign-up sheet with your newsletter.
3. Send home volunteer sheets as needed for tasks.
4. Have a parent organize all the volunteers.
5. Work with the PTO or PTA to obtain ideas on how parents can help.

Tips on Acknowledging Volunteers

1. Send home thank-you notes after a completed event.
2. Host a special parent volunteer luncheon.
3. Have students write thank-you notes at the end of the school year or term.

4. Invite parents to the classroom for a special play and social gathering.
5. Place names of parent volunteers who helped during the week in your weekly newsletter.

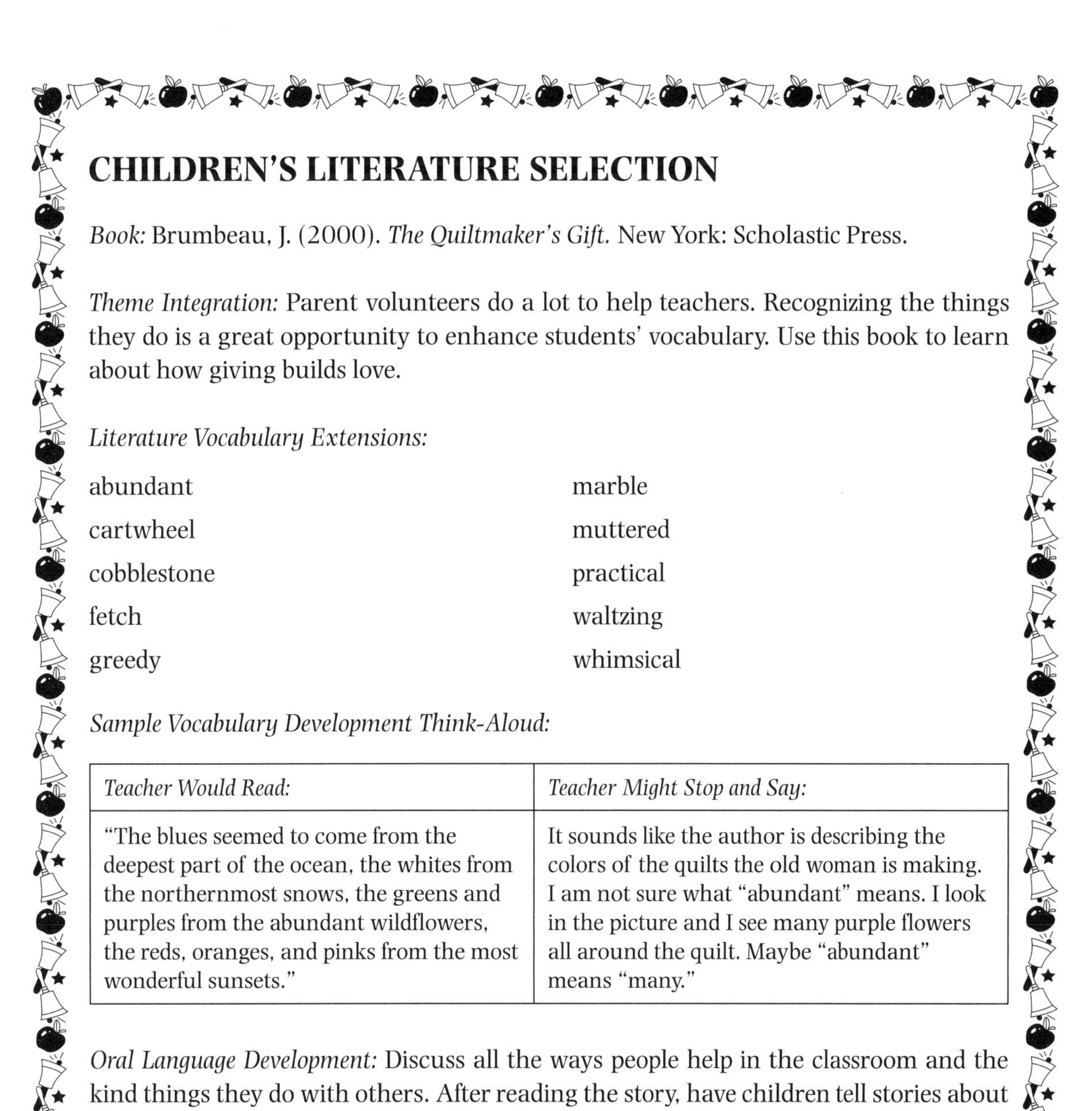

CHILDREN'S LITERATURE SELECTION

Book: Brumbeau, J. (2000). *The Quiltmaker's Gift.* New York: Scholastic Press.

Theme Integration: Parent volunteers do a lot to help teachers. Recognizing the things they do is a great opportunity to enhance students' vocabulary. Use this book to learn about how giving builds love.

Literature Vocabulary Extensions:

abundant
cartwheel
cobblestone
fetch
greedy
marble
muttered
practical
waltzing
whimsical

Sample Vocabulary Development Think-Aloud:

Teacher Would Read:	*Teacher Might Stop and Say:*
"The blues seemed to come from the deepest part of the ocean, the whites from the northernmost snows, the greens and purples from the abundant wildflowers, the reds, oranges, and pinks from the most wonderful sunsets."	It sounds like the author is describing the colors of the quilts the old woman is making. I am not sure what "abundant" means. I look in the picture and I see many purple flowers all around the quilt. Maybe "abundant" means "many."

Oral Language Development: Discuss all the ways people help in the classroom and the kind things they do with others. After reading the story, have children tell stories about kind things they have done for their parents. Select a word from the extension list that students need to learn more about and see if one person can use that word in his or her story. During story sharing, students can listen to hear the selected word.

2

Oh, the Words We Know!

Teaching vocabulary to primary grade children is essential. Previous studies of reading vocabulary (word meaning) using story books in the primary grades reported gains of 20%–30% of word meanings taught.

~Biemiller & Boote (2006, p. 44)

THEME REFLECTION

Alphabetic knowledge is the process by which students are capable of knowing that each speech sound or phoneme of a language should have its own distinctive graphic representation (Harris & Hodges, 1995). Recall that phonemes are the smallest sound unit that represents spoken language. When the *Report of the National Reading Panel: Teaching Children to Read* (NICHD, 2000) was published, attention was directed to the alphabetic knowledge of primary grade students so that phonemic awareness of letters and sounds can be developed. According to the Early Reading First initiatives established by the No Child Left Behind legislation, it is apparent that children entering kindergarten have an awareness of alphabetic knowledge.

Early childhood centers of excellence integrate the alphabetic principle in literacy and do not treat it as an isolated skill. This means that children's literature plays an important role in enabling young readers to develop knowledge of sound-letter associations. According to Ehri (1995), children develop the alphabetic principle through stages. Primary grade children differ from each other in developmental levels and therefore will not all be at the same stage at the same time.

Stage 1—Pre-alphabetic: Children recognize words using visual cues. Alphabet books can be used to demonstrate picture, sound, and letter relationships. What teachers can do to help develop pre-alphabetic skills is to use mnemonics, which are pictorial cues for letters of the alphabet. Many children's picture books integrate ABCs with pictorial cues to help children remember their alphabet.

Stage 2—Phonetic Cue Reading: Children begin to use partial sound recognition in words, such as initial sounds or final sounds. During this stage, students are able to begin distinguishing the differences in letters and the sounds they make. Students begin to internalize certain letters that are meaningful to them. During this stage, teachers can use many interactive reading books that make sounds or play musical chants to help students remember the ABCs.

Stage 3—Full Alphabetic: Children are using all letters of a word to try to make sense of the word. When reading stories, do picture walks first, and during the read-aloud, stop to see if children can say the next word in the text. Have children describe pictures and the words they might find in the book, write down the words, and then say them together.

According to the research by Biemiller and Boote (2006), there are specific strategies that teachers can use to increase vocabulary development based on children who are preliterate (are not yet reading) or literate (can read) readers. For preliterate children, vocabulary is best learned when others read to them. Literate children should stop and ponder or ask about things they do not understand. Words they ask about can be placed on a list for subsequent attention. Literate children take more responsibility when trying to learn new words. Words that children learn best are words that are meaningful in their lives. Words that children use in writing act as a baseline for word learning allowing further vocabulary to develop naturally from the child's personal knowledge base.

LIST #9 WITTY WORDS WE KNOW FROM A TO Z

The 25 words in this list are words that tend to be a bit tricky for students because of distinct sounds and letter associations. Many of these words are used less frequently, but are also considered to be subject words that are difficult to learn.

asked
balloons
cookies
dance
excited
fuzzy
guess
hobby
inside
juice
know
liberty
might
number
other
pink
quiet
room
socks
turn
until
visit
warm
yes
zoo

Journal Writing Prompts

My friend likes the three words ___, ___, and ___ because...

Pink is...

While at the zoo, I saw...

Vocabulary Literacy Scaffolds: Based on the findings of Biemiller and Boote (2006), use the words above to help preliterate students gain confidence with familiar words and ABC sound-letter associations. Students can read the words in pairs and place them in alphabetical order. In their journals, have them list the alphabet from A to Z and write as many of the words as they know from the list above. After they list each letter of the alphabet, have them write new words with the same beginning sounds. They can refer back to their list when writing.

CHILDREN'S LITERATURE SELECTION

Book: Seuss, Dr. (1963). *Dr. Seuss's ABC.* New York: Random House.

Theme Integration: Every classroom probably has a copy of *Dr. Seuss's ABC.* This book will help students at varying levels build confidence with vocabulary and word learning.

Literature Vocabulary Extensions: Words on this list are found in the book.

alligator
bubbles
camel
doughnuts
elephant
feathers
fox
goggles
hen
itchy
jelly
kettle
lion
mice
necktie
ostrich
pajamas
queen
rhinoceros
sick
turtles
umbrella
violin
washes
young
zizzer-zazzer-zuzz

Sample Vocabulary Development Think-Aloud: (Note: If students have a copy of this book, have them bring it to school to share with other students.)

Teacher Would Read:	*Teacher Might Stop and Say:*
(Before you begin reading, read aloud the list of words that have been selected for each letter of the alphabet. Invite students to participate if they know the word.) "BIG A / little a / What begins with A?"	What do you think begins with the letter _______? Have students finish the prompt using the correct alphabet word on the list.
Continue reading through the book.	Invite children to respond before you read each page.

Writing Development: Dr. Seuss books are a great resource to encourage writing and vocabulary development. Have students work in pairs to create their own Dr. _______ book. Begin with the same prompts in the book, but finish using other words they wrote on the list of ABCs from their journal.

LIST #10 WORDS WE USE WHEN WE GO PLACES

This list includes 10 words that can be used to explain places children like to go. Presented after each core word are additional extension words that have similar meaning.

dinner—**feast,** banquet, formal dinner, buffet

farm—ranch, farmhouse, barn, bungalow

game—sport, match, competition, diversion

hayride—festival, fair, carriage, wagon

movies—**show,** production, cinema, film

party—bash, celebration, gathering, festivity

room—area, space, section, region

school—college, university, academy, institution

swing—slide, **monkey** bars, tire, merry-go-round

zoo—circus, spectacle, extravaganza, exhibition

Journal Writing Prompts

Make a list of your favorite places to go.

Make a list of your family's favorite places to go.

Make a list of the places you wish you could go.

Vocabulary Literacy Scaffolds: Students love writing about the places they like to go. Everyone wants to tell a story about a favorite place. Use this motivation to inspire kids to learn many different ways of naming or referring to their favorite places to expand their vocabulary. Invite students to add to this list.

CHILDREN'S LITERATURE SELECTION

Book: Seuss, Dr. (1990). *Oh, the Places You'll Go!* New York: Random House. This book will inspire children and adults to think positively about what they are doing and where they are going.

Theme Integration: This book is a classic book for many students who have to deal with change. Use this book at the beginning of the school year, or at the start of a new semester to talk about the many places you will go. This can mean "going places" in books, too!

Literature Vocabulary Extensions:

Far-off lands . . .

Distant places . . .

Sample Vocabulary Development Think-Aloud:

Teacher Would Read:	*Teacher Might Stop and Say:*
Oh, the Places You'll Go!	Where have you gone this past . . . ? Tell your neighbor what it was like to go to this place. Where are we going to go today when we read this story?

Oral Language Development: While reading this book, when a new place is discovered, add it to the list above. When you are done, ask children to describe what each place looks like. Have them choose a place on the list, draw a picture, and use new words to explain this place.

LIST #11 DR. SEUSS FUN

Below is a list of words that children can use when talking about Dr. Seuss books.

biggest
brother
candy
happy
presents
sister
surprise
tree
Who

Journal Writing Prompts

Use the words above to create a new story. For example, Presents left under the tree were for my brother but . . .

Who . . .

Vocabulary Literacy Scaffolds: The list above includes nine words. Invite students to add to this list all the other words they know that they might find in Dr. Seuss books. Place silly words in a different list, but include them.

CHILDREN'S LITERATURE SELECTION

Book: Invite children to bring their favorite Dr. Seuss book to school. Alternatively, you can check several out from the school library and make them available for the children.

Theme Integration: Dr. Seuss books are a great place to remind students of the words they do know and use that prior knowledge to create new words and learn synonyms and antonyms for the familiar words.

Sample Vocabulary Development Think-Aloud:

Teacher Would Say:	*Teacher Might Stop and Say:*
Okay everyone, now it is your turn to read your books and discover more Dr. Seuss words. Find a partner with a book you like. Before reading your book, make a list of words you think you would read in the book.	Students, now it is your turn to begin reading. Begin by asking your partner questions about the book and the words on the list. Next begin reading. We will start with (group) to show us what to do.

Writing and Language Development: After reading the books with a partner, have two groups of two join to form groups of four. Now have the groups share all the new words they learned. Children should explain why the words are new. If time is limited, give them a specific number to share. For example, tell them to share one to three words each.

LIST #12 NAME GAMES

This list includes many of the different names students use to identify people.

angel
aunt
babies
baby
brother
cousin
dad
daddy
family
friend
grandma
grandpa
mom
mommy
nurse
people
police
Santa
sister
stylist
teacher
uncle
witch

Journal Writing Prompts

Using a class list of names, have students write something special about each classmate after his or her name.

Vocabulary Literacy Scaffolds: Names are very important to children. They like to write about people they love and about their classmates. Make sure names of all students are prominently displayed. Include everyone's name on your word wall with a picture of each student. Distribute a class list to all the students. Give them one copy to place in their journal. (Tape it to the front inside cover.) Send another copy to keep at home.

CHILDREN'S LITERATURE SELECTION

Book: Nolen, J. (2006). *Plantzilla Goes to Camp.* New York: Simon & Schuster. This book is about a silly looking plant girl who goes to camp. She writes letters to important people she knows and tells them about her adventures.

Theme Integration: This book logically follows a previous list on important places (see List #10). In List #12, you learned about important names students use to identify people. Before reading this story, increase students' background knowledge of letter writing. Show them letters you have written, or have them bring from home letters that they have received.

Literature Vocabulary Extensions: (This book is filled with rich vocabulary. Each page has new words that children will have fun learning. I have selected theme words that describe people or places, but there are many extension words that can be introduced.)

bully
camper
caretaker
counselors
discovery
forest
getaway
guardian
hike
island
lake
mountains
nature
parent
pen pals
slugger
superintendent
travel
vacation
woodsy

Sample Vocabulary Development Think-Aloud:

Teacher Would Read:	*Teacher Might Stop and Say:*
(Read one of the sample letters.)	Who knows how to write a letter? What is included in a letter? Does anyone know what a pen pal is? How many of you have gone to camp?

Writing and Vocabulary Development: This book has so many different possibilities for writing and word learning. Consider having class pen pals in science class, and have students begin to grow their own plants. Invite children to write letters to their pen pals about their plants. Make sure they describe such things as where their plant lives, how many siblings it has, and whether or not the plant likes to travel. Invite the children to make a list of all the questions they could ask using words from the lists in this chapter.

LIST #13 MY WORD WALL

Have students make their own Personal Word Walls using a file folder. On the outside, write the child's name and the title "My Word Wall." The purpose of making a Personal Word Wall folder is so the reader can put words that are familiar to him or her on the list.

On the inside of the folder, have students write the letters of the alphabet. After each letter, they can write down familiar words they already know. As they learn new words, they can add the words to the list under the beginning letter sound. An example is below.

A—**angel** B—**brother** C—**cousin** D—**daddy**

Vocabulary Literacy Scaffolds: The purpose of this Personal Word Wall is to give students a place to put words they really like to use. Give students a list of the core words and have them select words to put in their folders as in the example above.

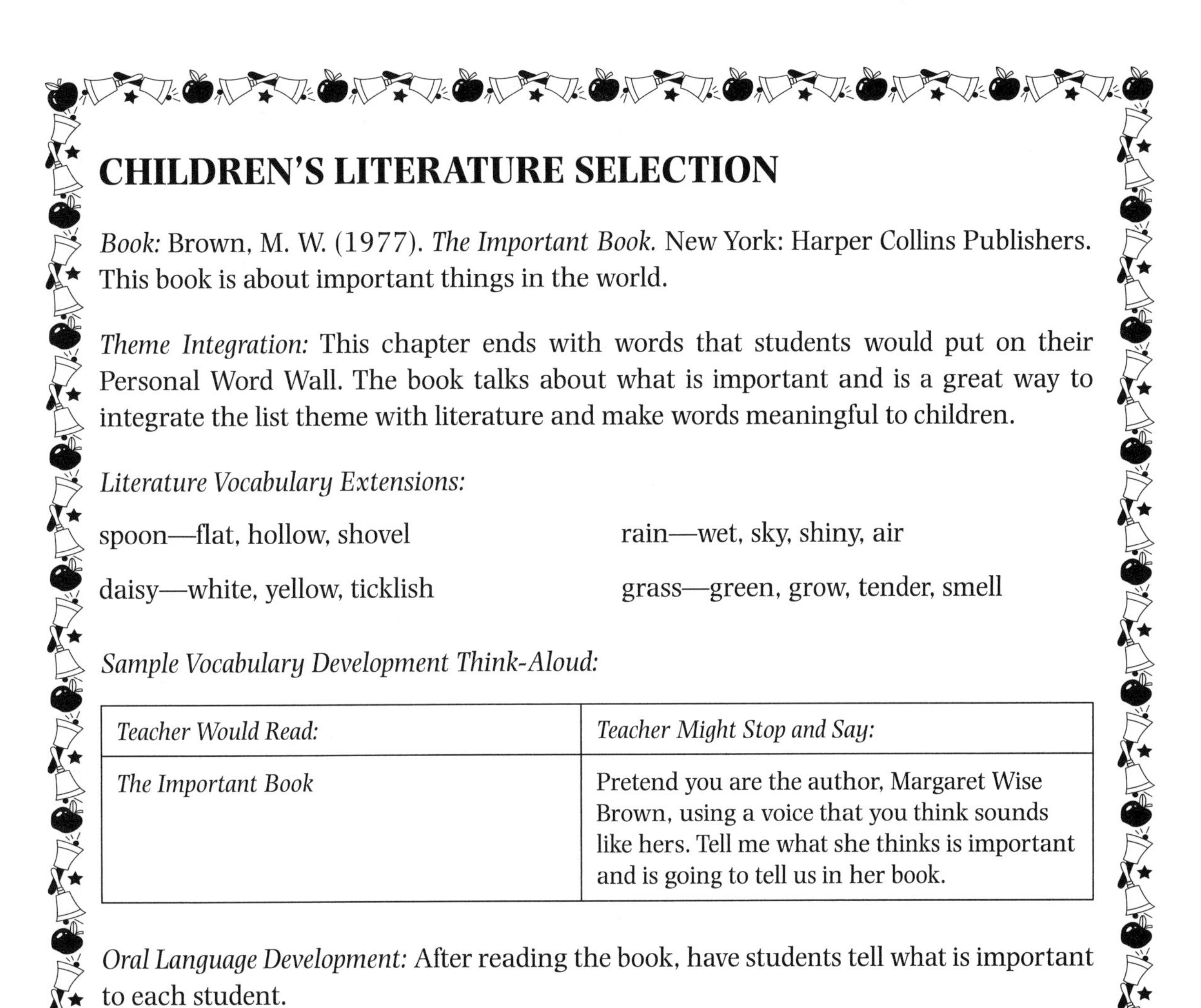

CHILDREN'S LITERATURE SELECTION

Book: Brown, M. W. (1977). *The Important Book.* New York: Harper Collins Publishers. This book is about important things in the world.

Theme Integration: This chapter ends with words that students would put on their Personal Word Wall. The book talks about what is important and is a great way to integrate the list theme with literature and make words meaningful to children.

Literature Vocabulary Extensions:

spoon—flat, hollow, shovel

rain—wet, sky, shiny, air

daisy—white, yellow, ticklish

grass—green, grow, tender, smell

Sample Vocabulary Development Think-Aloud:

Teacher Would Read:	*Teacher Might Stop and Say:*
The Important Book	Pretend you are the author, Margaret Wise Brown, using a voice that you think sounds like hers. Tell me what she thinks is important and is going to tell us in her book.

Oral Language Development: After reading the book, have students tell what is important to each student.

LIST #14 ABC BOOKS RESOURCE LIST

Alphabet Books for Developing Beginning Reading Skills

ABC Picture Book Title	*Integrated Literacy Activity*
Extreme Animals Dictionary by Clint Twist	Inspire children to make extreme animal hand puppets out of paper sacks and construction paper. While reading the book, children can hold up their puppets when appropriate.
K Is for Kissing a Cool Kangaroo by Giles Andreae and Guy Parker-Rees	This is a fun book to help children understand that the alphabet letters have both capital and small forms. Using magnetic alphabet letters, while reading this book children can sort the letters in ABC order, as well as locate the small and capital letters.
Campbell Kids Alphabet Soup by Campbell's	This is a great book to read on a cold day. Plan to have alphabet soup for lunch, and while reading this book, children can try to find and eat letters in the alphabet.
The Disappearing Alphabet by David Diaz	This book has interesting hidden alphabet letters on each page. Invite the children to do a picture walk through the book first to see if they can find the alphabet letters. They will spend hours enjoying this book before you even get a chance to read it as a read-aloud. Once they have found the letters, have them write the letters on paper.
Ashanti to Zulu: African Traditions by Margaret Musgrove	When learning about different cultures, this ABC book can be used to teach vocabulary about things that are different in other countries. It is recommended this book be read a few pages at a time to allow for dialogic discussions.
America: A Patriotic Primer by Lynne Cheney	This book is special because it talks about America and is a wonderful book to use during important days in our history such as the Fourth of July or Presidents' Day. Before reading this book, write the letters of the alphabet on a chalkboard. Ask the children to talk about the letters of the alphabet and have them think of words beginning with each letter that have to do with America. Invite children to talk first to encourage oral language development. This book is also a Caldecott Book, so this would be a great opportunity to talk about the Caldecott Medal.

SOURCE: Israel (2008).

3

Phonics and Teamwork

One forgets words as one forgets names. One's vocabulary needs constant fertilizing or it will die.

~Evelyn Waugh

THEME REFLECTION

This chapter focuses on phonics skills that are frequently difficult for primary grade children to grasp. The lists and strategies presented will help students develop phonics skills. In addition, specific lists focus on "r-controlled" words, digraphs, and diphthongs. I have incorporated the theme of "teamwork" into this chapter because letters and sounds need each other to make the words.

The chapter includes a collection of visual prompts that teachers can use to help students identify unknown words. These sample flashcards are based on Clark's research (2004). Clark outlines a number of coaching cues teachers can try instead of the overused "Sound it out."

At the beginning of the school year, primary grades spend a lot of time on behaviors related to working together, or teamwork. It takes many people working together in the primary grades to get students off to a good start and for them to stay focused, especially when they are learning to read. Use this chapter to help you build the theme of teamwork in your classroom, while at the same time helping students learn about the difficult words that frequently occur in reading and writing.

LIST #15 WHAT TO SAY INSTEAD OF "SOUND IT OUT"

Instead of telling students to sound out words they are unable to decode, use the following Coaching Cue Cards for alternatives (Table 3.1). Action cues focus on the grapheme-phoneme, larger word parts, and contextual supports.

Table 3.1

Coaching Cue Card #1	Coaching Cue Card #2	Coaching Cue Card #3
What do you think that letter sounds like?	It's a ___ letter sound?	Is there a word part you know?
Coaching Cue Card #4	**Coaching Cue Card #5**	**Coaching Cue Card #6**
Can you take something off?	Look for a little word.	Look for a compound word.

SOURCE: Adapted from Clark (2004).

LIST #16 WORDS WITH R-CONTROLLED VOWELS

Teachers should understand that r combination for vowel control is neither long nor short. Teach the single vowel cards in the following order: e i u o a. Place the r card next to each vowel, beginning with the e. The r is the boss but polite: he lets the vowel go first. The following list can be used when teaching r-controlled words with students

er words

her stern term jerk nerve

perch fern verse

ir words

birds **third** skirt thirsty dirty squirm **squirt** firm dirt

sir fir chirp mirth sir **girl** shirt

ur words

burn nurse purse **turn** fur curt spur lurk

surf church

or words

for nor **born corn fort** horn **porch** port sort

storm thorn cord fork stork scorch

ar words

bar car par jar tar **farm** arm hard barn harp

card bark **shark park** yard darn yarn

Journal Writing Prompts

I like the farm because...

___ gave the purse to the ___ and...

My fort is made of...

Vocabulary Idea Share: Work with the students to complete a journal prompt. Place several finished prompts on the board. Using the flashcards from List #15, work with a small group of any children who are having trouble with digraphs, and use the student-generated sentences to help the students learn how to read the words. Use the flashcards as prompts to guide students when they struggle with a word in the sentences.

CHILDREN'S LITERATURE SELECTION

Book: Cronin, D. (2003). *Diary of a Worm.* New York: HarperCollins. This story is about a worm who keeps a diary. In his diary, he records his observations during the day.

Theme Integration: The book helps students put r-controlled words with text that is easy for them to read.

Literature Vocabulary Extensions:

art
dangerous
dinner
forget
garbage
hard
her
homework
park
service
turn
very
worm
worst

Sample Vocabulary Development Think-Aloud:

Teacher Would Read:	*Teacher Might Stop and Say:*
Diary of a Worm	Has anyone seen a worm before? Do you like to eat worms? What other words rhyme with worm?
"April 15th: I forgot my lunch today. I got so hungry that I ate my homework."	What did the worm eat for lunch? Why? What words on this page have an "r" sound? Let's write those words on the board and see if the author uses them again.

Oral Language Development: When you are finished reading this book, invite students to recall all the r-controlled words they heard throughout the story. Make a list of all the words. Reread the story with the class to see if they missed any words. Check comprehension by having them ask you questions about the worm.

LIST #17 THE "H" BROTHERS

A former first-grade teacher of 33 years helped me understand digraphs. She called them the "h" brothers. This list is organized around consonant combinations with the letter "h." Introduce the word digraphs by calling them the h brothers. Review voice placement for these sounds: th wh ch sh.

Digraph th	*Digraph wh*	*Digraph ch*	*Digraph sh*
bath	**what**	chair	bash
than	**when**	chalk	**fish**
thank	**where**	chess	mash
the	**while**	chest	sash
their	**white**	chicken	share
them	**who**	child	**she**
then	whole	children	shelf
thin	whom	**chimney**	shell
thing	**why**	coach	shine
think		much	ship
third		such	**shoe**
this		touch	**short**
those			shot
thousand			**show**
with			wash

Journal Writing Prompts

The children playing chess by the chair . . .

Show me the shell you found near the . . .

Why do you think three . . . ?

Vocabulary Idea Share: To help students remember how to say words with consonant "h," tell them a story. First ask, What is your last name? Then tell them about the h brothers and how their last name ends in "h." You can begin the story like this: "Everyone, do you know that I have a brother whose last name is . . . ?"

CHILDREN'S LITERATURE SELECTION

Book: Fox, M. (1997). *Whoever You Are.* New York: Harcourt Brace.

Theme Integration: The title of this book helps students place digraphs in context with other words that are meaningful. The title also will remind children of the importance of knowing who we are, which will inspire them to remember the story about the h brothers.

Literature Vocabulary Extensions:

their
whoever
wherever

Sample Vocabulary Development Think-Aloud:

Teacher Would Read:	*Teacher Might Stop and Say:*
"Little one. Who are you?"	Think about who you are. Why did your parents give you your name? Think about where you are from.
"Little one, whoever you are, wherever you are, there are little ones just like you all over the world."	How can other people be just like you?

Oral Language Development: After reading this beautiful short story, invite children to recall the "wh" words. Then have them use the words they recall in sentences one at a time to tell a story. For example, using a "wh" word, a student would begin the story by saying, "Wherever I go . . ." The next student can finish the sentences or continue with the story. All the students will add something. This book can be read by students in the class as a choral reading once the class finishes the group story.

LIST #18 COW WORDS

When working with vocabulary words that are considered diphthongs, it is important that the teacher understand the concept of the word and its definition. It is less important that the student who is learning to read know what a diphthong is. A diphthong is a sound that glides from one vowel or consonant to the next making no other sound like it in the alphabet. Since there are not that many words that contain diphthongs, it is helpful for students to know how to read the words early in their reading development. This list contains vowel diphthongs.

au—fault, caught, daughter, taught, laundry, vault, fault

ew—few, pew, threw, screw, stew, chew

oi—soil, spoil, toil, foil, boil, coil, oil

oo—**look, took,** shook, **good,** igloo, broom, **school**

ou—**house, out, outside, our, hour, cow**

ow—owe, known, row, yellow

oy—royal, toy, **boy,** joy

ue—true, clue, glue, **blue**

ui—suit, cruise, fruit, **juice**

(Additional vocabulary resources from Green and Enfield, 1974.)

Journal Writing Prompts

If I were a royal . . .

The yellow . . .

In my house, there was a . . .

Vocabulary Idea Share: Have students place the above diphthong vowel combinations and words on index cards. Children can sort the words into the appropriate diphthong category. Once the words are sorted, students can create sentences with words in each category. Students can write sentences in journals or on the chalkboard to use as a culminating review activity.

CHILDREN'S LITERATURE SELECTION

Book: Cronin, D. (2000). *Click, Clack, Moo: Cows That Type.* New York: Simon & Schuster. This book is about exactly what the title says: cows that type. The cows in the barn type letters to the farmer to explain their problems.

Theme Integration: Give a concrete example of the sound "ou" that you hear in diphthong words and how the vowel sounds blend together. The story will help your students remember the /ou/ sound in "cow."

Literature Vocabulary Extensions: Begin with one word, such as "cow," and have students think of rhyming words to extend their thinking. Make a list of the words; after reading this story, have the children use a rhyming word to tell a new story.

Sample Vocabulary Development Think-Aloud:

Teacher Would Read:	*Teacher Might Stop and Say:*
Click, Clack, Moo: Cows That Type	What is going to happen in this story? Can this story really happen? If you were a cow, what would you tell the farmer in this story?

Oral Language Development: Give students an opportunity to respond to your questions above before going on to finish the story. Write some of the answers on the board. With older students, you can use their responses as journal writing prompts.

PART II

Read-to-Me Words

Building Rich Vocabulary Through Storybooks and Other Print-Rich Materials

Events in the past decade have changed the way many educators think about values that guide children's educational and literacy development in the twenty-first century. September 11, 2001, changed the way many of us think about our role as reading teachers. We more thoughtfully evaluate what we give children to read, how we teach them to read, and what we hope they gain from their reading. Other events, such as the humanitarian efforts that aided victims of the Asian tsunami and Hurricane Katrina, and political efforts that support international peace initiatives, have also increased the need to reflect on teaching practices in general and, more specifically, teaching practices related to reading instruction. Because of the changes in our nation and in our world, attention has shifted from a teacher-centered approach to literacy learning to a more student- or learner-centered approach. Likewise, the way authors are writing children's literature is also changing.

Children develop vocabulary by listening to adults read to them. The word lists in this section focus on words that children might encounter during a storybook read-aloud experience. The children's literature selected for each list extends the chapter's theme and incorporates research-based strategies that will develop vocabulary during storybook read-aloud experiences.

Primary Grade Teachers' Resource Toolbox: Vocabulary Instructional Resources, Theory to Practice

Storybook Circles

Cole, A. (2003). *Knee to Knee, Eye to Eye: Circling In on Comprehension.* Portsmouth, NH: Heinemann. Teachers who want practical strategies for integrating comprehension strategy instruction with storybook reading will find this a valuable resource. Children in the primary grades love to sit on the floor and listen to stories while they develop comprehension.

Comprehension Strategies

Duffy, G. G. (2003). *Explaining Reading: A Resource for Teaching Concepts, Skills, and Strategies.* New York: Guilford Press. This is another valuable resource that explains many comprehension strategies. The author shares years of his research with children in classrooms where words ands storybook reading are valued.

Balanced Vocabulary Instruction

Pressley, M. (2006). *Reading Instruction That Works: The Case for Balanced Teaching* (3rd ed.). New York: Guilford Press. The author of this popular book explains the most recent research on vocabulary instruction in elementary classrooms, and the importance of teaching vocabulary in authentic approaches through reading and writing.

4

New Genres

It is the ability of learners to think on their own and to evaluate and create that is the sign of educational success. It is the ability of a child to engage in the search for truth that is the sign of educational progress.

~Patricia McCarthy

THEME REFLECTION

The new genre of children's picture books is the postmodern picture book. The postmodern picture book resembles a book written like no other. As I started trying to bring some of the new children's literature into my undergraduate course titled "Foundations of Literacy Through Literature," I began to realize that it was becoming increasingly difficult to place some of the new books into the old genre categories. Genres that I taught when I was a teacher—mystery, fantasy, and biography—were being replaced with much more sophisticated children's picture books. The new genres of children's literature are published in a variety of creative ways with different formats, multiple perspectives within a story, multiple genres, and multiple types of writing styles. In order to help my preservice teachers learn about how to integrate the new genres in their instruction on children's literature, I started to create my own categories that seem to better identify the types of postmodern picture books being written. The vocabulary words in this chapter are organized around these new genres. As children's literature begins to change, the types of vocabulary change. The lists in this chapter are related to new genres and include the following types:

- Children's literature that develops reflective thinking
- Children's literature that encourages collaboration and participation
- Children's literature that supports humanity
- Children's literature that incorporates new literacies and technology

The new genres listed above will be described in more detail at the beginning of each of the word lists. The children's literature selected in this chapter will help teachers begin to learn about the new types of books, and it will help them develop strategies to increase vocabulary and word meaning with primary grade children. The multiple meaning constructions within the children's literature being written today will be addressed with the vocabulary selections, activities, and children's literature explained in this chapter.

LIST #19 WHAT ARE YOU THINKING?

This list focuses on words that children use when explaining their thoughts or constructing meaning. Sometimes children's lack of vocabulary to explain what they are thinking might keep them from wanting to speak. The words on this list will help develop children's reflective thinking. The activities here also provide the background knowledge of children's literature related to developing reflective thinking.

excited	eager, thrilled, impatient, enthusiastic
favorite	choice, desire, alternative, option
fun	amusing, enjoyable, terrific, super
guess	deduce, presume, assumption, theory
like	similar, represent, indicate, pleasing
mean	denote, indicate, relate, infer
remind	repeat, memory, mind, reminiscent
see	vision, image, dream, apparition
surprise	shock, astonish, amazement
tell	inform, **know,** explain, enlighten

Discussion Prompts

What words can you use to explain your thoughts?

Do you wonder why sometimes it is hard to tell others what is on your mind?

Does your parent ever ask you what you are thinking? What do you say?

Vocabulary Literacy Scaffolds: Pressley, M. (2006). *Reading Instruction That Works: The Case for Balanced Teaching* (3rd ed.). New York: Guilford Press. Pressley recommends that vocabulary be taught in natural environments. This part is about helping primary grade children develop increased vocabulary through storybook reading. Use this opportunity to immerse children in literature and explain to them the parts of the book. Introducing children to dictionaries is also a good way for them to expand their vocabulary. If they see you using a dictionary, they will become very curious and want to learn more.

CHILDREN'S LITERATURE SELECTION

Book: Garland, M. (2005). *Miss Smith's Incredible Storybook.* New York: Puffin Books. This story is perfect to introduce transitioning primary grade students from oral language vocabulary development to learning vocabulary from storybooks. Children will be inspired to read this book, if only because of its interesting plot and creative illustrations.

Theme Integration: Characters in the book come to life, inspiring students to think metacognitively.

Literature Vocabulary Extensions: Words on this list are found in the book; they were also selected to help children explain their thoughts.

adventure
amazement
chaos
character
fright
life
middle breeze
pounding
problem
story
thought
trouble
wondered

Sample Vocabulary Development Think-Aloud: (Note: If students have a copy of this book, have them bring it to school to share with other students.)

Teacher Would Read:	*Teacher Might Stop and Say:*
"It was the first day of school. Zach was waiting for his teacher to arrive. Boring, boring . . . he thought. Why would this year be any different from the last one?"	Think about your fist day doing something new. Was that day boring to you? Why do you think Zach had a boring year at school last year?
"Then the door swung open. 'Good morning, class. My name is Miss Smith, and I am your new teacher.'"	Look at the picture of Miss Smith. Do I remind you of Miss Smith? What do you think Miss Smith is going to read in the book she is carrying?

Writing Development: After reading the story, have the students pick one of the characters that came to life and write a story about that character reading a book to the class. If students are not yet old enough to write stories, have them tape-record their stories using character names and the new words on this list to explain what happens. Children can listen to each other's stories in centers.

LIST #20 BOOKS WITH LESSONS

This list provides the background knowledge for building vocabulary that will help your students identify with children's literature that is related to books that encourage collaboration and participation. Characteristics of books in this genre include interactive books, paired reading books, multiple version books, and visual imagery books. The words on this list reflect how primary grade children might speak to each other when working in groups. This list also teaches these children how to use language to show respect for others.

acknowledge
contribution
cool
effort
engage
give
group
input
interact
involve
kind
like
listen
nice
participate
pleasant
please
polite
practice
proud
share
thank
together
turn
welcome

Journal Writing Prompts

A time when I worked well with others was . . .

Together we . . .

Reading together is . . .

Vocabulary Literacy Scaffolds: To help students make connections with the words on this list, have them write a list of paired reading rules. First, instead of using the word "rules," tell children their first task is to figure out a different way to say "rule." I offer more words below. This will help children learn more words as well as understand that working together should stem from habit and not from a rule.

Synonyms for the word *rule:*

code
doctrine
guidelines
habit
law
policy
practice
routine
tenet

Figure 4.1 Ideas on helping children make connections with words about working together

---

Paired Reading Guidelines

1. Be kind to reading pair.
2. Take turns.
3. Listen and acknowledge in a polite manner.

CHILDREN'S LITERATURE SELECTION

Book: Hoberman, M. (2004). *You Read to Me, I'll Read to You: Very Short Fairy Tales to Read Together.* New York: Scholastic. This is a book that can be used with paired reading. Each fairy tale includes two colors of text on each side of the page identifying when the next reader is to begin reading.

Theme Integration: This interactive storybook helps children with comprehension strategies. It helps them work together to develop reading ability and increased vocabulary.

Literature Vocabulary Extensions: Since this book has so many repeated words, I am using the names of the characters on the extension list.

Baby Bear
Big Bad Wolf
Billy Goat
Cinderella
Duck
Fairy Godmother
Hen
Jack
Little Red Hen
Little Red Riding Hood
Mister Ogre
Pea
Pigs
Princess
Queen
Stepsisters
Troll

Sample Vocabulary Development Think-Aloud: (Note: If students have a copy of this book, have them bring it to school to share with other students.)

Teacher Would Read:	*Teacher Might Stop and Say:*
"Introduction / Here's another book, Book Two. You read to me! I'll read to you! / We'll read each page to one another. You'll read one side, I the other."	This is a different book where two or more can read together. Let me show you how to read this book with your partner. Who would like to help me?
The Three Bears "I'm Goldilocks"	(Student volunteer reads) I'm Baby Bear

Reading Development: Model the first story for students. Children can read the book in pairs during reading time. Rereading the same story changing characters is encouraged.

LIST #21 WE ARE SPECIAL

The words in this list provide the background knowledge to help children understand that vocabulary is used to explain the similarities and differences among people. The children's literature used to make connections with the words on this list support the new genre related to books that discuss humanity. Books in this genre have the characteristics that reflect stories that are related to crisis-oriented struggles students might face, real-life issues such as divorce or death, and stories about special needs children. Children in primary grades like to write about people who are special to them. The words in this list are different ways of conveying the meaning "special." Let children decide which words are too challenging for them to remember, but at least give them the opportunity to hear different ways to explain how people in their life are special.

bright
brilliant
different
distinguished
essential
exceptional
extraordinary
important
individual
key
outstanding
unique
unusual
vital

Journal Writing Prompts

I am special because...

The person in my life who is...

My teacher is...

Vocabulary Literacy Scaffolds: Create a "We Are Special" bulletin board. Have students bring a picture to class to place on the board. Invite students to cut out words in magazines to stick by the pictures of students in their class. Once the board is full, which might take a month or so, let the students take their pictures and the vocabulary words that their classmates used to describe why they are special.

CHILDREN'S LITERATURE SELECTION

Book: Curtis, J. L. (2002). *I'm Gonna Like Me: Letting Off a Little Self-Esteem.* New York: HarperCollins.

Theme Integration: This book helps children discover what is special about them.

Literature Vocabulary Extensions: Words on this list are found in the book.

brave
bunch
fad
grin
head
last
mistake
mouth
myself
sharing
straight
stretch
style
teeth
wrong

Sample Vocabulary Development Think-Aloud: (Note: If students have a copy of this book, have them bring it to school to share with other students.)

Teacher Would Read:	*Teacher Might Stop and Say:*
"I'm gonna like me wearing flowers and plaid. I have my own style. I don't follow some fad."	I love wearing plaid, especially in my favorite colors blue and green. Who is wearing plaid today? Does anyone know what a fad is?
"I'm gonna like me when I climb on and wave as the bus pulls away and I'm feeling so brave."	What's going on in this picture? Where are the children going? How many children in the picture are wearing plaid?

Vocabulary Development: Finish the sentence, "I'm gonna like me . . ."

LIST #22 WIRED WORDS

This chapter provides the background knowledge on words that children use when working on or with technology. The children's literature for this list was selected to provide an example of how to incorporate new literacies and technology themes. Children's literature related to new literacies and technology comes in the form of CD-ROM storybooks, hypertext, digitally influenced books, and other technology media. The words in this list were selected to help children use familiar vocabulary to write effective e-mails.

Top nine function words:

and	**the**
I	**to**
is	**we**
it	**you**
my	

Words to write more effective e-mails:

all	said
am	sincerely
are	**so**
because	**take**
but	**their**
dear	**them**
did	**there**
do	**they**
from	**today**
had	**too**
has	**what**
have	**will**
off	**would**
on	

E-mail Writing Prompts

Dear Mom and Dad . . .

Today at school . . .

Thank you for . . .

Vocabulary Literacy Scaffolds: More and more children use the Internet to communicate. The words in this list will help students write more effective e-mails with fewer words misspelled. Use this opportunity to teach other words students know about technology and the Internet. Make your own class list and keep it with the Personal Word Wall words. It might help students to distinguish student-generated words from the Word Wall words.

browser
CD
display
Internet
keyboard
laptop
mouse
printer
software

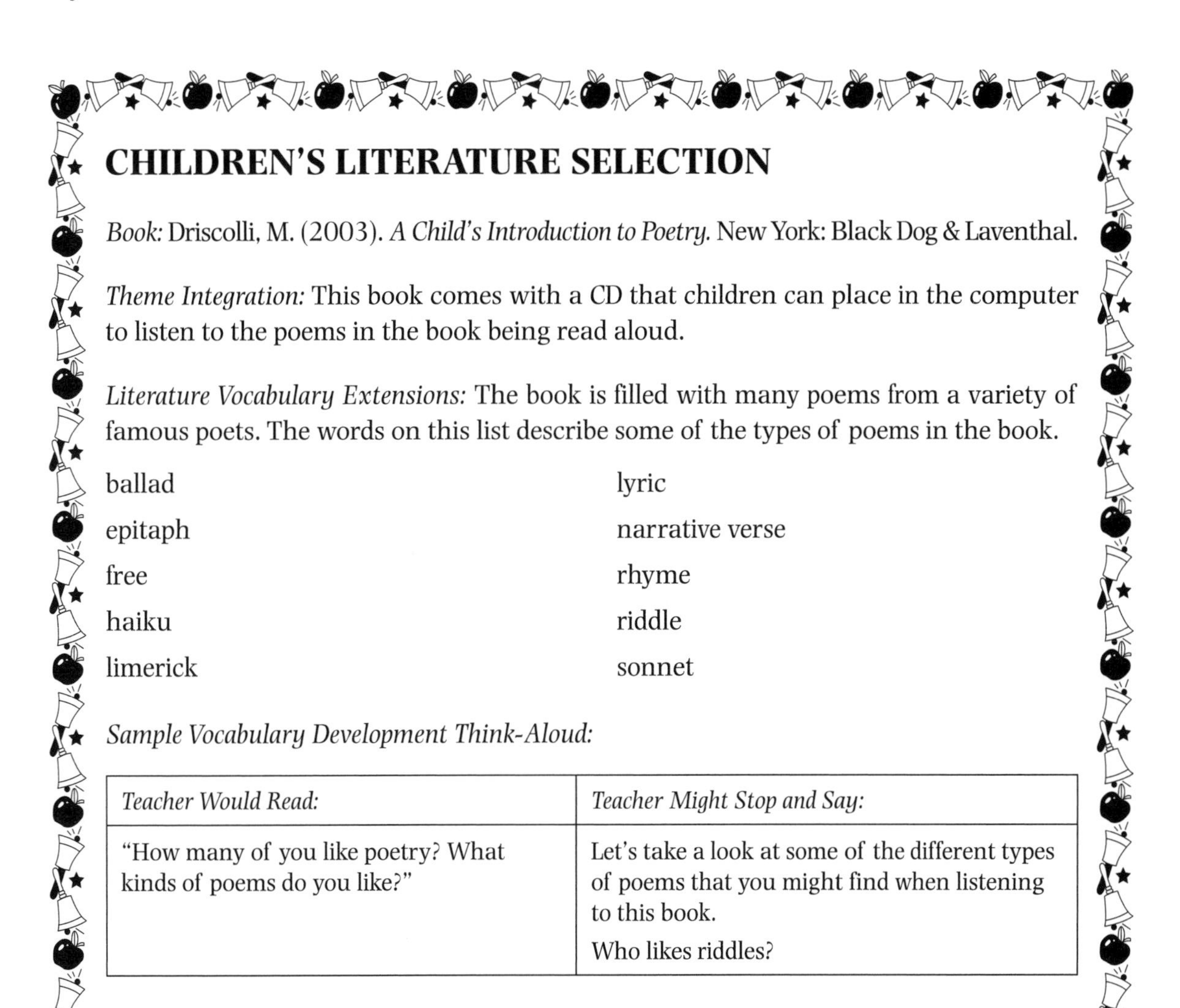

CHILDREN'S LITERATURE SELECTION

Book: Driscolli, M. (2003). *A Child's Introduction to Poetry.* New York: Black Dog & Laventhal.

Theme Integration: This book comes with a CD that children can place in the computer to listen to the poems in the book being read aloud.

Literature Vocabulary Extensions: The book is filled with many poems from a variety of famous poets. The words on this list describe some of the types of poems in the book.

ballad
epitaph
free
haiku
limerick
lyric
narrative verse
rhyme
riddle
sonnet

Sample Vocabulary Development Think-Aloud:

Teacher Would Read:	*Teacher Might Stop and Say:*
"How many of you like poetry? What kinds of poems do you like?"	Let's take a look at some of the different types of poems that you might find when listening to this book. Who likes riddles?

Writing Development: This book and word list are perfect to begin writing poems using the word processor as a writing tool. After you identify some of the children's favorite types of poems, practice writing their favorite types with words they have learned thus far. Refer back to their Personal Word Wall folder and have them begin creating a poem using any style they choose. Use this time to join them in writing poetry of your own.

LIST #23 "WORDS I KNOW" WEB

One reading strategy that can be integrated when developing new vocabulary words and reading children's literature is reviewing and revision. It is important to begin to develop the concept of "review and revise" at an early age. This would be a good point to go back through all the word lists and make a list of words that students know and words that they still need to learn. Your list can be developed around a "Words I Know" web.

Directions: Use the "Words I Know" web, and add words to the diagram as a class. The web can be enlarged on bulletin board paper so students can add words that they know.

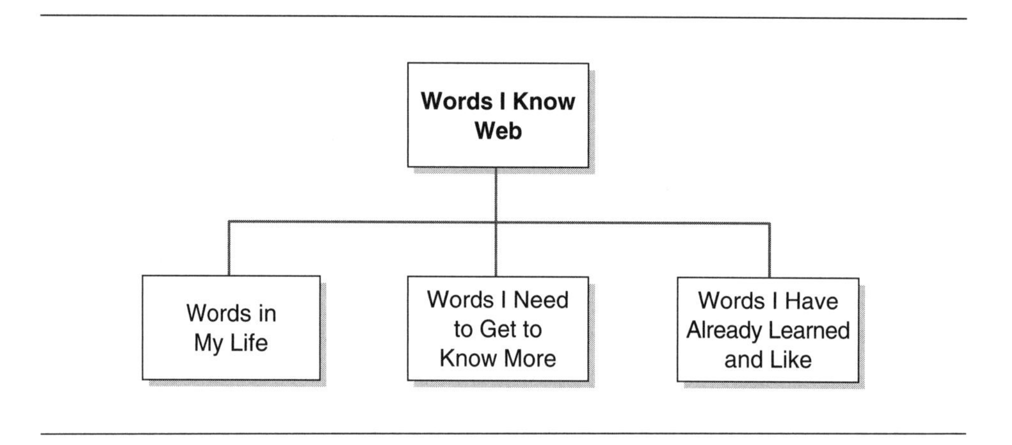

5

Informational Storybooks

T. Lee Williams
Auburn University

Knowledge is of two kinds. We know a subject ourselves, or we know where we can find information on it.

~Samuel Johnson

THEME REFLECTION

No matter how long you teach, there are always a handful of students that you will never forget. These memorable students stand out because of a uniqueness of spirit that touches something inside of us. For me, Nicholas was one of those students. From the very moment I met him on the first day of fourth grade, Nicholas's love for dinosaurs was apparent. In fact, after I introduced myself to him he immediately asked me a question: "Mrs. Williams—true or false? The Tyrannosaurus rex had two fingers on each hand?" This line of true/false questioning on all things dinosaur became a yearlong conversation starter each time we talked. I learned more about dinosaurs that year from Nicholas than I ever imagined was possible. Nicholas is an excellent example of an info-kid (Jobe & Dayton-Sakari, 2002), a student who is interested in facts. The type of knowledge that Nicholas has about dinosaurs is a great example of Samuel Johnson's two types of knowledge that starts this chapter. Nicholas knew where to find information on dinosaurs because that was the only type of book he checked out all year. And after so much reading on the subject, Nicholas internalized much of the information. To reach children like Nicholas, we must include nonfiction in our reading programs. This chapter focuses on themes related to nonfiction, which can be used to broaden a child's vocabulary on topics that are truly interesting to the child. And for those who are wondering, the answer is true—the Tyrannosaurus rex had two fingers on arms that were only about three feet long.

LIST #24 NONFICTION FOR EVERYONE

There is a growing interest in including more nonfiction in the primary grades. Teachers and researchers alike are realizing that many students prefer nonfiction to fiction. Recently, publishers have responded to this interest; as a result, there are many excellent nonfiction books now available. The words on this list are some that students may encounter when reading on a wide variety of nonfiction topics.

animals
away
ball
bath
bone
care
cow
dog
drink
excited
farm
fish
food
fuzzy
get
going
home
horse
house
hungry
I
is
it
jump
like
love
monkey
my
name
newspaper
our
outside
pets
puppy
shark
sit
toys
treats
water
we

Journal Writing Prompts

My favorite animal is ___ because...

My favorite hobby is ___ because...

My favorite thing to study in science is ___ because...

Vocabulary Literacy Scaffolds: Students need to understand the world around them and that many disciplines use specific language. Send this list home to parents when you begin a new science study, and invite them to read the list with their primary grade child so he or she can become familiar with the language of nonfiction.

CHILDREN'S LITERATURE SELECTION

Book: Blackaby, S. (2003). *A Dog for You: Caring for Your Dog.* Minneapolis, MN: Picture Window Books.

Theme Integration: The focus of this book is on caring for a pet dog. The book uses engaging artwork to complement the important information about dogs. Web sites and books for further reading are included.

Literature Vocabulary Extensions:

clean
crate
exercise
leash
legal
shedding
shelter
training
treats
veterinarian
water

Sample Vocabulary Development Think-Aloud:

Teacher Would Read:	*Teacher Might Stop and Say:*
"Your dog needs a safe place to sleep. A dog can nap in a crate. It can doze in a basket."	I'm not sure what the word "doze" means. Let me read further.
"Your dog can snooze on a rug. It can curl up with you."	Oh, now I think I know what the word "doze" means. It means the same as nap and snooze. Who knew there were so many great words to use for sleep!

Oral Language Development: At the middle of the book, stop and invite children to share experiences they have had with their own dogs. Reinforce using new words as they tell their stories.

LIST #25 COOKBOOK FUN

Children love to cook. Whether it's at home or in the classroom, there are so many skills that can be integrated with cooking. Following directions, measuring, and reading for a purpose are three skills that are naturally a part of reading a recipe. The words on this list are some that children will encounter when they cook. If you've never cooked in your classroom, give it a try—your students will love it!

ate
bake
bananas
beans
bowl
brown
can
cook
cooked
cooking
cooks
counter
dessert
eat
eating
eggs
family
favorite
feast
fish
food
hamburger
juice
lunch
make
makes
mashed
milk
minutes
next
off
oven
pan
pizza
potatoes
restaurant
sugar
sushi
thermometer
treats
turkey
warm

Journal Writing Prompts

Let me tell you about a terrific recipe that my ____ makes . . .

My favorite thing to cook is . . .

The best cook I know is . . .

Vocabulary Literacy Scaffolds: In order for students to learn to cook, they must be familiar with the most common words associated with cooking. Send this list home to parents when you are planning to cook in the classroom, and invite them to read the list with their primary grade child so he or she can become familiar with the language of cooking.

CHILDREN'S LITERATURE SELECTION

Book: Wilkes, A. (1997). *Children's Quick and Easy Cookbook.* New York: Dorling Kindersley Publishing.

Theme Integration: This is a terrific cookbook for children! It is organized by types of cooking: snacks, meals, desserts, and treats. There is a wonderful introduction containing kitchen safety information, and the entire book boasts amazing pictures to support step-by-step instructions.

Literature Vocabulary Extensions: The words on this list are words that can be found in the book.

barbeque
cutting board
drain
ingredients
knives
omelet
oven mitt
pasta
peel
recipe
sauce pan
smoothie
spatula
trim

Sample Vocabulary Development Think-Aloud:

Teacher Would:	*Teacher Might Stop and Say:*
Copy the title to a recipe from the book, "Cheater's Pizza," onto an overhead transparency so that all students can see.	Does anyone know what a cheater's pizza is? How could we find out?
Read all the ingredients and then the steps of the recipe.	I don't see a definition, but I think it might be called a cheater's pizza because we're using an English muffin for the crust.

Oral Language Development: After reading the book, ask students what other ingredients could be used for the crust in the cheater's pizza (e.g., hamburger buns, bagels, etc.).

LIST #26 BUGS AND BRAINS

Young children love bugs! And an excellent way to teach the life cycle is through the story of the butterfly. The words on this list are some that children will encounter when they read books about bugs.

air	**how**
animal	**inside**
are	**know**
bones	**legs**
built	**live**
butterfly	**long**
called	**looking**
camouflaged	**middle**
climb	**name**
collecting	**need**
flower	**night**
fly	**outside**
garden	**park**
green	seen
have	**sleeping**
hide	**small**
home	**trees**

Journal Writing Prompts

My favorite bug is . . .

I have these questions about the butterfly.

If I could create a bug, it would ___ and it would look like this . . .

Vocabulary Literacy Scaffolds: In order for students to be successful in school, they need to understand the world around them. Connecting with students' interest in the natural world helps to bridge the known with the new. Send this list home to parents when you study about bugs, and invite them to read the list with their primary grade child so he or she can become familiar with the language of entomology.

CHILDREN'S LITERATURE SELECTION

Book: Jeunesse, G., & Delafosse, C. (2004). *Butterflies.* New York: Scholastic Books.

Theme Integration: The focus of this book is on the life cycle of the butterfly.

Literature Vocabulary Extensions: The words on this list are words that can be found in the book.

caterpillar
chrysalis
crunch
eggs
fuzzy
nettle leaf
pasture
pupa
skin
spin
wriggle

Sample Vocabulary Development Think-Aloud:

Teacher Would Read:	*Teacher Might Stop and Say:*
"One last time the caterpillar shakes itself and sheds its old skin. But this time, the caterpillar's new skin in different. It is tight and stiff. It is now called a pupa."	Does anyone know what a pupa is? Let me read further.
"For two weeks the hard pupa does not move. It looks like a shriveled leaf. But the dull pupa case is a hiding place. Inside the caterpillar is changing."	Oh! So a pupa is sort of like a shell for the caterpillar. It protects the caterpillar while it's changing into a butterfly.

Oral Language Development: At the middle of the book, stop and invite children to use the vocabulary that is specific to butterfly development. Have students share with the group and explain the most interesting word they heard and what it means to them. Reinforce using new words as they tell their stories.

LIST #27 FACTUAL FUN

Many children love facts and will go to any length to learn everything there is to know about a certain subject. Dinosaurs, trains, geography, and world records are just a few subjects that come to mind. The words on this list are some that children will encounter when they read factual books.

about
aren't
around
be
been
believe
best
did
don't
ever
first
great
guess
have
last
lots
never
old
person
run
say
short
started
team
than
their
went
who
won
year

Extension words:

carnivore
dinosaur
extinct
fact
herbivore
paleontologist

Journal Writing Prompts

The subject I know most about is . . .

If I could set a world record, it would be for . . .

The most interesting thing about dinosaurs is . . .

Vocabulary Literacy Scaffolds: Send this list home to parents, and invite them to read the list with their primary grade child so he or she can become familiar with the language of fact-based reading.

CHILDREN'S LITERATURE SELECTION

Book: Scott, J. (2002). *Discovering Dinosaurs.* Minneapolis, MN: Compass Point Books.

Theme Integration: The focus of this book is on facts about dinosaurs. The book includes wonderful photographs of fossils as well as Web sites where children can find more information.

Literature Vocabulary Extensions:

carnivores
defense
detective
discover
fossil
herbivores
herd
museum
reptile
scientist
triceratops
Tyrannosaurus rex

Sample Vocabulary Development Think-Aloud:

Teacher Would Read:	*Teacher Might Stop and Say:*
"Different dinosaurs had different defenses against enemies."	What do you think the word "defenses" means in this sentence? Let me read further.
"Some had spiked tails, horns, hard plates, and claws. Some were fast runners."	Oh, now I think I know what the word "defenses" means. It means the way that the dinosaurs could protect themselves.

Oral Language Development: At the middle of the book, stop and invite children to share some of the interesting facts about dinosaurs they've learned from the book. Write the student-generated facts on chart paper. Add to the chart at the conclusion of the book. Reinforce using new words as the children tell their stories.

LIST #28 CULTURAL CURIOSITY

Art, music, drama, and dance are all areas that children are very interested in, but they are often considered "extras" in the school day. Try incorporating more culture in your classroom through reading! The words on this list are some that children will encounter when they engage in reading books on the arts.

because
best
class
dance
danced
enjoy
finger
friend
fun
going
guitar
happy
hop
I
I'm
is
it
jump
like
love
mirror
music
my
paint
pink
play
playing
practice
proud
school
shoes
sing
the
times
to
trophy
watch

Journal Writing Prompts

The instrument I would most like to learn to play is the . . .

The time I saw a live dance or music performance, it was . . .

My favorite artist (dancer) (musician) is . . .

Vocabulary Literacy Scaffolds: Incorporating the arts is a wonderful way to reach even the most reluctant readers. Supplement your curriculum by integrating reading in your arts program. Send this list home to parents, and encourage them to read the list with their primary grade child so he or she can become familiar with the language of the arts.

CHILDREN'S LITERATURE SELECTION

Book: Bray-Moffatt, N., & Handley, D. (2003). *Ballet School.* New York: DK Children.

Theme Integration: This how-to book on ballet provides a step-by-step explanation of important ballet positions and techniques.

Literature Vocabulary Extensions:

arabesque
ballerina
barre
body
leotard
muscle
performer
pliés
pointe
position
shoes
studio

Sample Vocabulary Development Think-Aloud:

Teacher Would Read:	*Teacher Might Stop and Say:*
"The ballet class takes place in a large studio."	I wonder why it's called a studio. Let me read further.
"There are full-length mirrors on one wall to check your positions and a special wooden floor that springs a little when you jump so that it will not be too hard on your feet."	Oh, now I think I know what the word "studio" means. A dance studio looks very different from an artist's studio.

Oral Language Development: After reading the book, invite children to share any experiences they have had in a dance class. Reinforce the vocabulary.

6

Celebrations

Of course, knowledge is never static or complete. A leader who is through learning is through. You must never become satisfied with your ability or level of knowledge.

~John Wooden (Wooden & Jamison, 2005, p. 100)

THEME REFLECTION

According to Pressley (2006), interest plays a role in motivation and literacy development. Relative to interest and literature selections, Pressley writes,

> Interest can affect both attention and learning, but only some of the increases in learning are due to its effect on attention to academic content. . . . We should not dismiss the possibility of increasing student interest in what they read. . . . I think we need to think hard about how to increase access to books and magazines that are attractive to kids as well as how to make worthwhile readings more attractive to elementary students. (p. 390)

Interest also plays a large role in motivating students to be metacognitive and engaged in reading tasks. According to Griffith and Ruan (2005), one of the roles played by interest and metacognition in literacy instruction is the relationship between attention and deeper processing. Before students can become metacognitive during processing, they need to be able to concentrate on what they are reading. One way to increase interest at the beginning of a reading task is to elicit think-alouds, set goals, activate prior knowledge, and offer reading materials that students value. Certain characteristics of text can also decrease student interest. For example, text that is much too difficult for the students to process, or text that does not adequately explain difficult concepts or terms, can cause students to lose interest. In addition, if students do not have adequate background knowledge of the text's subject, their interest levels decrease.

Creating interest at the beginning of a reading task by helping children understand vocabulary cultivates literacy learning in a way that helps them make sense of text. Vocabulary can be used as a way to create interest in literacy by

- Previewing words in advance
- Predicting word meaning
- Questioning or wondering how and why the author will use the words in the text
- Activating prior or relevant knowledge of familiar words and word associations
- Determining reader goals on building vocabulary
- Contemplating the purpose for reading and learning new words to increase interest levels in the task of reading and writing

Primary grade children love celebrations, especially celebrations related to literacy tasks they are learning about in school. This chapter uses celebrations to increase vocabulary and literacy learning. Celebrations increase student motivation and interest level. In addition, when students know about celebrations, the "anticipation of the celebration" becomes a motivation for learning. The words in this list are associated with things that primary grade children might celebrate in school.

LIST #29 HAPPY BIRTHDAY

Children love to celebrate their birthdays. They also like to let others know they are special on their birthdays. The words in this list are related to birthday celebrations.

balloons
birthday
cake
candy
cookies
excited
favorite
happy
laughed
party
present
surprise
toys

Related words:

age
anniversary
bingo
cheer
chocolate
cupcakes
favors
gift
ice cream
invitation
old
sing

Journal Writing Prompts

My birthday is on . . .

I would like a . . .

My favorite birthday gift was a ___ because . . .

Vocabulary Literacy Scaffolds: Invite students to bring in pictures of birthday celebrations. Using the words from this list, have them write about their most recent birthday. Students can make another list to generate more vocabulary words of favorite presents they have received. The list of words can be placed by their photo to create a Beginning of the School Year bulletin board.

CHILDREN'S LITERATURE SELECTION

Book: Have students bring in a book that celebrates birthdays, or a book they have made on their birthdays or family celebrations. The purpose of this is to share literature and cultures.

Theme Integration: This book can be read when talking about birthdays and celebrations. The words on this list are from the book.

Literature Vocabulary Extensions: Invite students to make a list of new words from the stories they read or shared in class.

Sample Vocabulary Development Think-Aloud:

Teacher Would:	*Teacher Might Stop and Say:*
Say, "Let's read the title of your book."	What type of questions would you like to ask _____ about his special day?
Read a passage from the book the child has selected.	Does this remind you of your birthday celebration? Tell me about it.

Reading Development: Have students sit in small groups of three or four and invite them to share their books with each other. Have them ask questions about their classmates' birthdays. The students will be very excited to talk about their birthdays. When you are finished, decide how they can celebrate others' birthdays in a special way. Consider connecting this to a service-learning project and make birthday cards for children who are in foster care.

LIST #30 CELEBRATING THE 100TH DAY

Primary grade children enjoy counting up to the one hundredth day of school. This is also a great way to help children integrate math and literacy vocabulary words. This list can be used to stretch children's imaginations when children have learned their numbers and are familiar with counting.

I have 100 of these in my bedroom and . . .

angels
bananas
basketballs
cars
flowers
monkeys
monsters
pillows
potatoes
rainbows
shoes
snowballs
socks
tags
turkeys
videos

Math Related Writing Prompts

If I had 100 ___, I would . . .

One day when I went outside to . . .

My neighbor is 100 years old and . . .

Vocabulary Literacy Scaffolds: Begin to introduce children to the concept of doing research. Using the Internet, see if they can find out how other cultures celebrate 100 days, or how other countries say 100. Have them generate a list of new words from their research that you can use on the 100th day. Invite children to print pictures if they find something interesting related to their new words.

CHILDREN'S LITERATURE SELECTION

Book: Slate, J. (1998). *Miss Bindergarten Celebrates the 100th Day of Kindergarten.* New York: Dutton Children's Books.

Theme Integration: Celebrations and the 100th day of the school year.

Literature Vocabulary Extensions: Different ways to read and write 100.

Sample Vocabulary Development Think-Aloud:

Teacher Would Ask:	*Teacher Might Stop and Say:*
What day is it today?	How many more days do we have left?
What do you think will happen in this story?	Tell me your ideas and we will see what happens next.

Oral Language Development: One way to practice new and learned vocabulary is using 100 index cards. Have the class help you write down all the words they know. Give them the cards and let them sort them by theme. To get ideas on sorting you can help them understand what a theme is. After the cards are sorted by theme, hang all the cards in the hall by the theme categories created by the students in your class.

LIST #31 HOLIDAYS

Schools enjoy taking time to celebrate holidays. This list integrates words associated with each holiday. Invite the children to include words they know from diverse cultures. Rather than telling students, give them an opportunity to rely on the cultural knowledge of the students in the class to figure out where they go on this list.

Asian **New Year**	dragon **dance, red** envelopes, fireworks, lanterns
Easter	**eggs,** bunny, basket, **candy,** spring, **bunch,** lilies, **park,** hunt
Cinco de Mayo	piñata, dancing, **parade,** mariachi
Fourth of July	**fourth,** fireworks, flag, **liberty, red, white, blue,** freedom
Halloween	**October, candy,** mask, spooky, monsters, **hayride, pumpkin, trick-or-treat**
Thanksgiving	**turkey, pie, potatoes, mashed, gravy, hungry,** dinner, **visited**
Hanukkah	menorah, candles, dreidel, gold coins, latkes, **gifts**
Christmas	**Santa, presents,** stockings, **tree,** ornaments, **snow,** snowflakes, **snowmen**
Kwanzaa	mat, **corn,** candles, kinara, **gifts,** unity cup, African culture

Journal Writing Prompts

My favorite holiday of the year is . . .

I picked up the piece of candy and inside was a . . .

My mashed potatoes landed on the . . .

Vocabulary Literacy Scaffolds: Using the concept of a Picture Walk, place the names of the holidays on the chalkboard and invite the students to add new words they know to the list. The next day, have the children bring in pictures that represent different things that would happen during that holiday. Place the pictures by the appropriate holiday and ask the children to see if they can generate more new words related to the pictures and that are also related to the holiday.

CHILDREN'S LITERATURE SELECTION

Book: Students' choice of a holiday book they would like to share.

Theme Integration: Celebrating diversity and the different traditions related to various holidays.

Literature Vocabulary Extensions: Invite students to find words in their books and write them on the chalkboard or on an index card. Use student-generated word lists to increase students' motivation and build on their prior knowledge.

Sample Vocabulary Development Think-Aloud:

Teacher Would Ask:	*Teacher Might Stop and Say:*
What is your book about?	Why do you think _______ culture celebrates in this manner?
What is your favorite holiday and why?	If you could create your own holiday, what would you call it and what would you do on that day?

Oral Language Development: Invite students to create a new holiday and celebrate that holiday using the student-generated word lists and the stories that you read in class.

LIST #32 SEASONAL FUN

This list includes the types of words that describe the seasons or what children might be doing during those seasons. Teachers can use this word list to have students generate more word lists based on what they do during each season or how they describe that season.

Summer words	**run, ball, zoo, water, blue, warm**
Fall words	**cool, football, climbed, tree, farm, ride,** orange
Winter words	**snow, outside, snowman, snowball, snow angels, snowy, gray**
Spring words	**basketball, rainbow, flower, green, swing, tag**

Journal Writing Prompts

My favorite season is . . .

I like to ___ in the ___ because . . .

My favorite season looks like . . .

CHILDREN'S LITERATURE SELECTION

Book: Edwards, J. A., & Hamilton, E. W. *Simeon's Gift.* New York: Harper Collins.

Theme Integration: Use this beautiful story to celebrate the many talents students have that they use during the different seasons. Inspire them to celebrate their gifts throughout the year. Note: This is a challenging book with a lot of vocabulary. You might want to consider reading this book over the course of several days so that students can become familiar with all the rich vocabulary in the book. I included my top 10 favorite words.

Literature Vocabulary Extensions:

castles
humble
lute
meager
monasteries
musician
pauper
rhythm
tapestries
villagers

Sample Vocabulary Development Think-Aloud:

Teacher Would Say:	*Teacher Might Stop and Say:*
Let's review the words that we might hear in this story.	What words have you heard before and where?
What other words do these words make you think of?	Let's think of as many words as we can and see if we hear them in the story while we are reading it.

Oral Language Development: When you are done reading a few pages, have students evaluate the book based on feelings. Begin to talk about the special talent of the minstrel.

LIST #33 LITERACY DAY

Use this list to invite children to think differently about literacy as an event that happens every day of the week. The words on this list were selected because are creative words that students can use when celebrating reading and writing in different locations and events.

class
downstairs
friends
hayride
home
inside
morning
outside
party
playing
pool
school
store

Journal Writing Prompts

Draw a picture of what literacy is for you.

Draw a picture of how you use literacy today.

Work with another student to draw a picture and write down what you want to do tomorrow related to reading and writing.

Vocabulary Literacy Scaffolds: Challenge students to make a list of what they would do related to reading and writing for each word above. This will help them think differently about literacy.

CHILDREN'S LITERATURE SELECTION

Book: Carle, E. (1997). *Today Is Monday.* New York: Scholastic. This book helps children realize the different days of the week and brings about new challenges.

Theme Integration: The focus of this book is on how literacy is present every day of the week. This story will challenge students to think differently about literacy.

Literature Vocabulary Extensions:

Monday
Tuesday
Wednesday
Thursday
Friday
Saturday
Sunday
weekday

Sample Vocabulary Development Think-Aloud:

Teacher Would Ask:	*Teacher Might Stop and Say:*
What day is it today?	What special literacy things have we done today in class?
What special literacy activities can you do every day of the week?	Explain when you might do this, or how this event makes you feel.

Oral Language Development: Use the book as a prompt to think of literacy that happens throughout the week. Invite students to make up their own silly rhymes using literacy as the theme. You can replace literacy for other words if you wish, such as writing, reading, thinking, or speaking.

PART III

How I Use Words I Can Read

Developing Vocabulary Literacy Through Writing

Children learn words in a developmental fashion. The vocabulary words in this section will provide students with opportunities to use words they know and can read to engage in writing. The children's literature enhances the theme. Instructional interventions provide opportunities for students to develop word learning through a variety of research strategies. In addition, the activities and strategies will help students begin to transfer the knowledge of learning words from reading to writing. Vocabulary development is important to writing development.

Primary Grade Teachers' Resource Toolbox: Vocabulary Instructional Resources, Theory to Practice

Word Learning Position Statements

The International Reading Association is the premier literacy organization that publishes research-based instructional resources. Teachers can visit their Web site at www.reading.org. The Association's parent resources include numerous vocabulary activities that can be found at www.readwritethink.org.

Looking Into Vocabulary Instruction of Exemplary Teachers

A model school for vocabulary development and instruction is the Benchmark School. Information about this school can be found at www.benchmarkschool.com. This school is based on research-based practices in vocabulary and reading comprehension, and it provides professional development for all teachers.

Children's Literature Favorite

Frasier, D. (2000). *Miss Alaineus: A Vocabulary Disaster.* New York: Harcourt. Both teachers and students can benefit from reading this book. Teachers can learn different ways to teach vocabulary. Students can learn how to remember the meaning of words.

7

Writers Learning New Words

Of course there are big differences in length and character and vocabulary, but each level has its particular pleasures when it comes to the words one can use and the way one uses them.

~Margaret Mahy

THEME REFLECTION

The purpose of this chapter is to provide teachers with words related to writing, and words that will help their students understand writing concepts and skills. Mahy's quote above gives insight into the pleasures students can discover as they learn more about how to use words and the many uses for them. According to the National Institute of Child Health and Human Development and the *Report of the National Reading Panel* (NICHD, 2000), greater emphasis needs to be placed on vocabulary development. There are three primary lessons that teachers can learn from this research and the primary word study we conducted. The first goal is for teachers to learn words as they are used by kindergarten through second grade students in the United States. The second goal is for teachers to learn about effective methods of building word skills and integrating word knowledge in students' writing. The third goal of the research is to make recommendations for instructional implications and future research that teacher researchers can engage in. Our study helps guide future research by suggesting that vocabulary instruction at the primary grade level should be studied in order to improve word-learning skills that can be integrated in writing so that writing skills can also improve systematically.

Primary Grade Vocabulary Teaching Tips

1. It is important to teach high-frequency words that children use in writing.
2. Encourage students to use words that are important to children—words they need to know to help them explain who they are and what they like.
3. Teachers who use seasonal themes in children's writing need to teach many seasonal words that are familiar to the children being taught. Teachers can generate a list of high-frequency seasonal words based on the words children already know.
4. Encourage students to be word detectives and invite them to generate lists of vocabulary words that would help them write interesting stories.
5. Teach primary grade children different ways to start sentences and stories. For example, instead of accepting all sentences that begin with "I," help children create more interesting sentences by starting with more descriptive words or subject words, as opposed to function words.

LIST #34 WRITER'S WORLD WORDS

This list provides students with basic writing words that they might hear or encounter when reading or when asked to write. This list can be displayed on a Personal Word Wall so that students can refer to it frequently. The list presents words that children might hear adults or teachers say; the word knowledge needs to be transferred to writing tasks so that students understand writing components. Teachers should use this list as a starting point and add other words they frequently use to explain writing as a task.

audience
author
beginning
chapter
character
conclusion
conversation
diary
end
idea
illustrator
introduction
journal
letter
middle
paragraph
phrase
plot
presentation
quote
sentence
setting
story
style
tone
voice
write
writer's workshop

Journal Writing Prompts

Writing is . . .

I like to write about . . .

My favorite writer is . . .

Vocabulary Literacy Scaffolds: Use the list to help students better understand the components of writing. Depending on the grade level you are teaching, or each student's ability level, place frequently used words to describe the various functions of writing on sticky notes. Using a book, point out to children how the words describe the parts of the writing and explain the function. For example, write the word "Introduction" on a sticky note and then stick it at the beginning of the story. Put the word "Conclusion" on a sticky note and show students where the conclusion is in the story.

CHILDREN'S LITERATURE SELECTION

Book: Stevens, J. (1995). *From Pictures to Words.* New York: Holiday House.

Theme Integration: This is a teacher's dream book for helping students transition from reading to writing. The book tells a story about the different parts that make up a story. The following key words are used in the book. The book also includes two pages that show what a storyboard looks like.

Literature Vocabulary Extensions:

adventure
authors
autograph
beginning
dummy
editor
end
fax
imagination
manuscript
middle
plot
printing
problem
publishing
revisions
rewrite
setting
story
storyboard
write

Sample Vocabulary Development Think-Aloud:

Teacher Would Read:	*Teacher Might Stop and Say:*
"From pictures to words."	This book is about making a book. What do you think the author is going to tell us in this story? Let's make a list of all the things you say and see if the author talks about them.
"Janet Stevens."	Who is the author of this book? What does an author do? Should we add these words to our list?

Writing Development: This book provides an excellent way to reinforce key concepts about writing. To check students' comprehension of writing words and meaning, ask each child to select a favorite book from your shelf or their desk. Do a check by saying some of the words in this list and the words the students suggested during your teacher think-aloud. Children should demonstrate that they understand by pointing to the word meaning or turning to a section. For example, say "author," and children should point to the name of the author of their book. Say "paragraph," and children should point to a paragraph in their story.

LIST #35 IDEAS FOR WRITING

When students have writer's block it usually means they do not have enough information on their subject. Students might say to you, "I don't know what to write about," or they might say, "I don't have any ideas." Begin using the words in this list to help students understand where they can locate information so they have more information on their subject. The words in this list refer to how they can gather new ideas.

book
city
experiences
family
friend
library
magazines
movies
people
school
teacher
vacations
world

Journal Writing Prompts

When I do not know what to write about, I can . . .

I get ideas about writing from . . .

I wish I could write about . . .

Vocabulary Literacy Scaffolds: To help students have ideas about writing, have them start a Writer's Idea Folder at the beginning of the school year or semester. See Table 7.1 for ideas on what to include in the folder. Using a file folder, have students write on the outside, "My Writer's Idea Folder." On the inside, have them collect writing ideas from a variety of sources. You can have students just place items in the folder, or you can have them organize their collections around important parts of a story.

Table 7.1 Ideas about what to collect for a Writer's Idea Folder

Character Ideas	*Plot/Problem Ideas*
animals	clothes
athletes	environmental concerns
cartoons	games
class list	international events
dancers	news articles
Disney characters	obituaries
faces	scenes from movies
fairy tale characters	space issues
family photos	things going on in politics
friends	unusual facts
presidents	unusual pictures
sports heroes	weather pictures
stars	

Setting Ideas	*Title Ideas*
antique shops	interesting words
barns	phrases
city	metaphors
farms	cool things people say
football stadiums	titles from newspaper articles
houses	quotes
interesting places	pictures that generate title ideas
maps	interviews
museums	list of favorite words
rooms	names
schools	
towns	
vacation photos	
zoos	

CHILDREN'S LITERATURE SELECTION

Book: Moulton, M. K. (2006). *Miss Sadie McGee Who Lived in a Tree.* Nashville, TN: Ideals Children's Books.

Theme Integration: Many children who have writer's block might need to take a break from their writing. Using books that inspire children to use their imagination when they write can help them generate new ideas. The words in this list rhyme, which will invite students to try to use words creatively. The pages in this book are unique. They will increase students' imagination because they fold out and make larger pictures. The illustrations in the book will also help children think creatively.

Literature Vocabulary Extensions:

beautifully
blissfully
certainty
contently
cordially
curiously
dizzy
graciously
happily
heavenly
inquisitively
journey
lucky
modestly
mystery
oddity
sea
see
silly
story
suddenly
tea
three
tree

Sample Vocabulary Development Think-Aloud:

Teacher Would Read:	*Teacher Might Stop and Say:*
"Tree"	What words rhyme with tree? What is it like to be in a tree?
Miss Sadie McGee Who Lived in a Tree	Use your imagination and describe Sadie McGee. Use words that rhyme with tree.

Oral Language Development: Children will have a lot of fun reading this book because many of the words rhyme and because the words are unusual. Have students read in pairs, taking turns turning the pages and reading. Invite them to create a song with the book. When done, go back to a writing assignment. Invite children to think of ways to describe their main character. Have them write down all the words they know that will describe this character. Invite them to return to what they were working on before they had writer's block.

LIST #36 WRITING PROMPTS

Primary grade students like to begin stories using writing prompts. Use this list to help students generate writing prompts that they can write down in their Idea Folders. When they have writer's block, have them return to this list. The words listed here should be used as the first word in a writing prompt. The activity below will help you inspire children to think of writing prompts.

clean	**today**
everybody	**tomorrow**
give	**we**
I	**where**
my	**why**
school	write

Vocabulary Literacy Scaffolds: This activity focuses on helping children write their own journal writing prompts. Invite children to use the words above to think of a writing prompt. For example, "I went to the story to buy . . ." Generate several writing prompts with the students. Have them copy the prompts in their Idea Folders. Next, have them work together with friends who have similar interests to generate more prompts.

CHILDREN'S LITERATURE SELECTION

Book: Grossman, V., & Long, S. (1991). *Ten Little Rabbits.* San Francisco: Chronicle Books, LLC.

Theme Integration: This book was selected to help teachers use literature as a way to inspire writing. The title of this book is from a favorite childhood rhyme, Ten Little Indians. Use favorite book titles, nursery rhymes, and poems to change the words and begin a new story. This list includes phrases from the book that can be used as writing prompts or story starters. This is an excellent book to integrate with a study on Native Americans or animals.

Literature Vocabulary Extensions:

Ten little . . .

One lonely traveler . . .

Two graceful dancers . . .

Three busy . . .

Four clever . . .

Five wise . . .

Six nimble runners . . .

Seven merry mischief-makers . . .

Eight patient anglers . . .

Nine festive . . .

Ten sleepy . . .

Sample Vocabulary Development Think-Aloud:

Teacher Would Read:	*Teacher Might Stop and Say:*
(Inside the cover) "Weaving, fishing, and storytelling are all part of this spirited book that celebrates Native American traditions as it teaches young children to count from one to ten."	Let's count from one to 10 together. Great, now what do you know about Native Americans? How do you think they count?
"The whimsical illustrations, reminiscent of Beatrix Potter, glow with brilliant color and are filled with fascinating detail."	I just read some very long words. Did you recognize any of the words I said. Whimsical . . . good. What does whimsical mean? What does the word reminiscent sound like to you? Does it remind you of another word? I like that you said remember, and remind, and scent. What do you think this word means now?

Oral Language Development: Reading the inside covers of books gives children an insight into how others explain books and will help them learn to use descriptive words when talking or writing. Continue talking about Beatrix Potter and her famous characters. Encourage your students to look for other books on Native Americans. When you are finished having this discussion, do a picture walk with the children and pay very close attention to what the bunnies are wearing. See if the children can discover the differences in blankets while you read the story. Invite them to read the numbers with you as you read.

LIST #37 CREATIVE WRITING CONNECTIONS

Children love to listen to stories so that they can set a goal of reading them independently on their own. As students get older, they will be asked to read something and write about what they read. This skill is usually called summarizing, or writing about the main idea or theme. Help the children make connections from reading about something to writing about it by using words that connect ideas. The purpose of this list is to help students transfer their thoughts to written form using more sophisticated words.

experience
explain
happen
interesting
like
made
mean
meant
memory
remind
similar
surprise
tell
think
understand
when
while
why

More ways to say the word *mean:*

denote
entail
imply
include
indicate
meaning
sign
signify
suggest

Journal Writing Prompts

The most interesting part of...

This story reminds me of...

I think the author was trying to imply...

Vocabulary Literacy Scaffolds: Have students select a word from the main list and use a thesaurus to discover new words. Show them how words are connected by using a graphic organizer as in Figure 7.1

Figure 7.1 Graphic organizer of word meaning connections

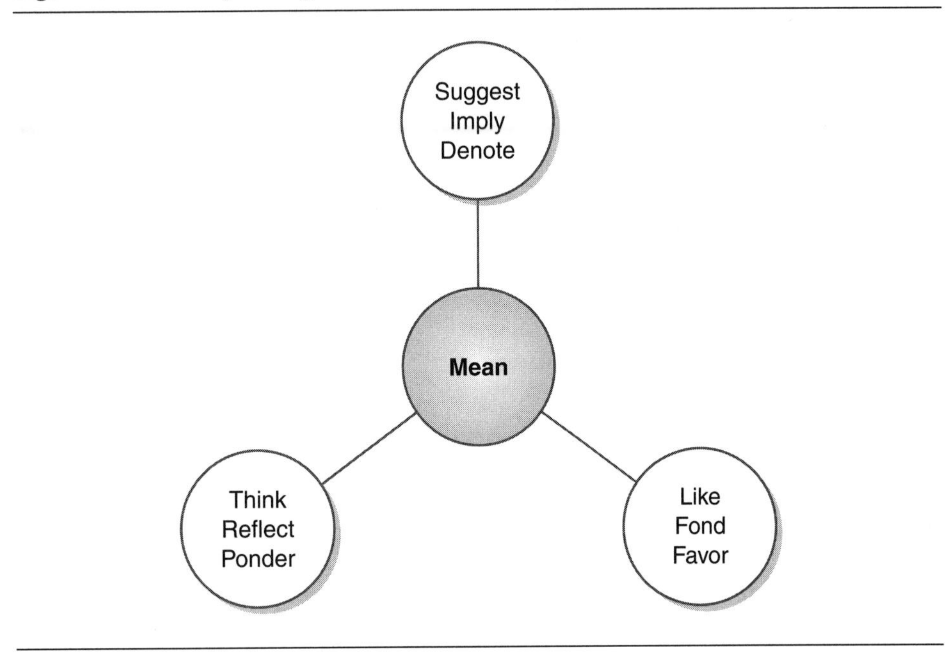

CHILDREN'S LITERATURE SELECTION

Book: Fox, M. (1985). *Wilfrid Gordon McDonald Partridge.* New York: Kane/Miller.

Theme Integration: This book will help students learn about memory. When going from reading to writing, students are expected to remember things and record their thoughts or feelings. This book will help teachers introduce the concept of making connections, and of reading comprehension as a skill.

Literature Vocabulary Extensions:

admired
favorite
knew
memory
precious
remember
secrets
told

Sample Vocabulary Development Think-Aloud:

Teacher Would Read:	*Teacher Might Stop and Say:*
	How do you remember what you read? What is a memory? What can you do to help you remember things from the past?
"The author is Mem Fox."	Who can remember other stories from this same author? (Teacher should have some books on display by the same author.)

Oral Language Development: Have students bring a sack of things from their past, which you can call a Memory Sack. Tell them to bring items that are very precious to them, just like in the story. In small groups, tell a story about the items in the sack. When the students are finished, have them write a story about the objects in their Memory Sacks.

LIST #38 VOCABULARY WORD LIST FROM ISRAEL AND FRY'S RESEARCH

The list below includes the words that primary grade students frequently use in their writing. It is based on samples of children's authentic writing. Hence, it is a list of words that children actually use when they are engaged in writing activities. This list will be useful to teachers when teaching writing or spelling.

Frequently Used Words by Primary Grade Students

a
about
across
after
again
air
all
also
always
am
American
an
and
angel
angels
animal
animals
another
any
anything
are
aren't
around
ask
asked
at
ate
aunt
aunt's
away
babies
baby
babysat
baby-sit
back
bag
bake
ball
bananas
bands
basketball
bat
bath
be
beach
beans
became
because
bed
been
behind
being
believe
belt
best
big
black
block
blond
blue
boat
bone
bones
born
bowl
boy
break
breakfast
bringing
broccoli
broke
brother
brother's
brothers
brought
brown
built
bunch
busy
but
butterfly
buy
buys
by

(Continued)

(Continued)

called	cooked	didn't	field
calling	cooking	do	fifth
came	cooks	dodged	fight
camouflaged	cool	doesn't	fights
can	corn	dog	finally
candy	could	doing	find
care	counter	done	finger
castle	couple	don't	fire
cat	cousin	dorm	first
cave	cousin's	down	fish
celebrate	cousins	drank	fit
ceremony	cow	drink	float
chasing	crane	drinks	floated
chimney	crown	eat	floor
chocolate	crushed	eating	flower
Christmas	crying	eggs	flowers
class	curly	eight	fly
claus	cut	elephant	food
clean	cut	end	football
climb	dad	enjoy	for
climbed	daddy	ever	forgot
climbing	dad's	evergreen	fort
clothes	dance	every	forth
cold	danced	everyone	four
coliseum	dared	everything	fourth
collecting	day	excited	French
color	dear	family	Friday
colors	December	farm	friend
come	decorate	favorite	friends
comes	degrees	feast	from
coming	dessert	feelings	fun
cook	did	fell	fuzzy

game	hamburger	hunting	looking
games	happen	hurt	lost
garden	happily	I	lot
gave	happy	if	lots
get	has	I'm	love
gets	haunted	in	low
getting	have	inside	lunch
ghost	having	is	mad
gift	hayride	it	made
girl	he	it's	mail
give	head	juice	make
given	hello	jump	makes
gives	help	jumped	making
giving	helping	kick	mall
go	her	kind	man
going	here	kindness	many
gone	hide	know	mashed
good	hill	landmark	me
good-night	him	last	mean
got	himself	laughed	middle
grandma	his	legs	might
grandmas	hockey	let	milk
grandpa	holiday	liberty	minutes
gravy	home	like	mirror
gray	hop	likes	miss
great	hope	little	mom
green	horse	live	mommy
guess	hot	lived	mom's
guitar	hour	lives	Monday
had	house	long	money
hair	how	look	monkey
half	hungry	looked	more

(Continued)

(Continued)

morning	off	pizza	reconciliation
motor scooter	oh	plant	red
mountain	old	plastic	reminds
moved	on	play	restaurant
movie	once	played	return
movies	one	playing	ride
music	open	please	road
my	or	pocket	rock
myself	other	polish	rolls
nail	our	ponytails	room
name	out	pool	rootbeer
named	outside	poor	run
names	oven	porch	sad
need	over	potatoes	sank
neighborhood	owl	pounds	Santa
never	owner	practice	Saturday
new	package	prayer	saw
newspaper	paint	present	say
next	pan	presents	saying
nice	papa	pretty	scared
nicer	parade	proud	school
night	Paris	pull	scored
nine	park	pumpkin	screamed
no	part	puppy	second
nobody	party	put	see
north	people	puts	seek
not	person	quarters	set
noticed	pets	quiet	seven
now	pie	rainbow	shark
o'clock	pilgrim	ran	she
October	pillow	ready	shoes
of	pink	really	shop

short
show
sick
since
sing
sister
sisters
sit
sitting
sixth
sixty
sleeping
slept
slid
small
smile
snow
snowball
snowman
snows
snowy
so
soccer
socks
some
somebody
someone
something
sometimes
sorry
sorts
spend
squirt
started
starts
statue
store
story
street
stuck
students
stuff
stuffed
stuffing
sugar
sun
Sunday
sushi
sweet
swim
swimming
swing
swinging
table
tae kwon do
tag
take
takes
talk
team
tell
ten
than
thank
thanksgiving
that
that's
the
their
them
then
there
thermometer
they
thing
things
think
third
this
those
three
thirty
throw
tick-tock
time
times
to
today
together
told
tomorrow
too
took
toys
treats
tree
trees
trick-or-treating
tried
trophy
trunk
tub
turkey
turn
tv
twelve
two
uncle
up
upon
us
used
uses
very
video
visit
visited
visiting
volcano
wait
waiting
want
warm
was
watch
watched
water
wavy

(Continued)

(Continued)

way	when	wishbone	ya
ways	where	witch	year
we	while	with	years
wear	white	woke	yet
Wednesday	who	won	you
weekend	why	words	your
went	wild	wore	you're
were	will	would	you've
what	win	wrapper	zoo

Generating Personal Word Lists: Have students use the following web to generate connections with words.

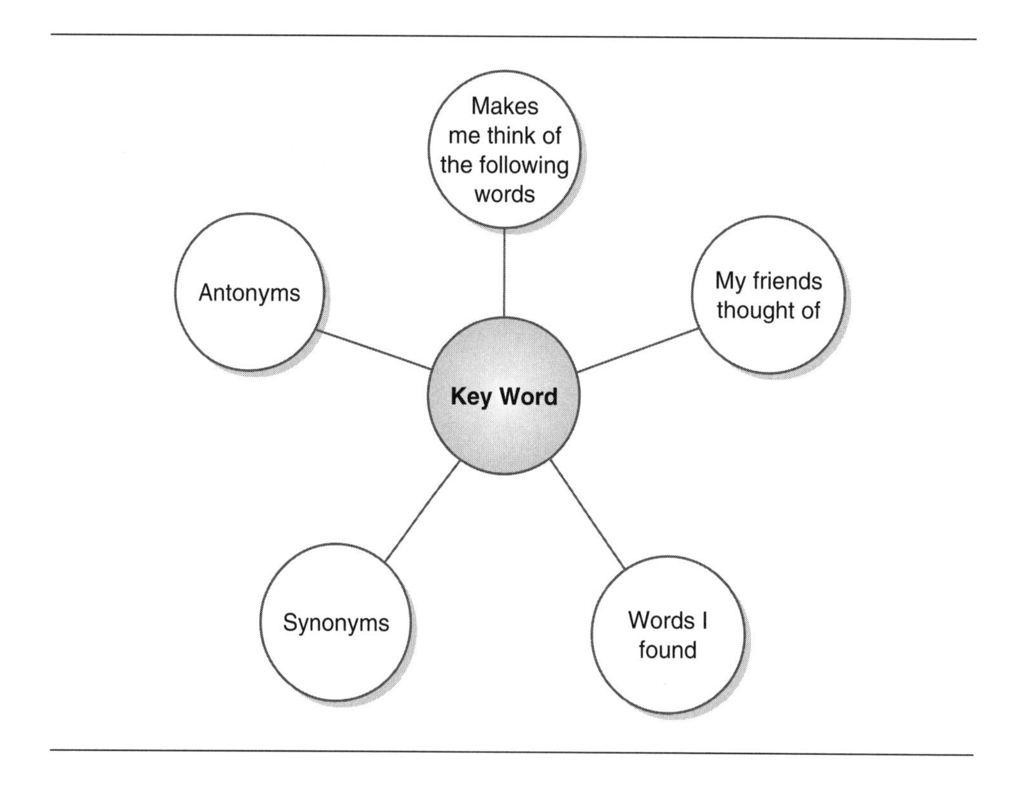

LIST #39 WRITING RESPONSES

Reading researcher Peter Johnston studied how teacher language impacts student achievement. In *Choice Words* (2004), Johnston explains how teachers' responses to students influence their motivation for learning. Inspired by Johnston's research, I developed the following list of ways teachers can respond to students' writing to help them improve their writing.

When responding to a story

Things you noticed

What you liked about the character

What other characters you are reminded of

A new idea you have about their character

What you found interesting

The talent they have with writing and how

What you saw in your mind as your read the story

Responding to writing that needs improvement or is not related to the assignment

This sounds interesting. Can you tell me more about . . . ?

You have a good start. Now finish it.

What do you notice about what you wrote that needs improvement?

I wonder if you considered . . . .

I would like for you to . . . .

Have you considered your audience?

How else . . . ?

What is a better way to say . . . ?

Can you extend . . . ?

Can you distinguish from . . . ?

How can we check this information?

Can you reread this to see if it makes sense?

Suggestions for students who are stuck or do not know what to write about

Can you look in your Idea Folder?

Consider interviewing someone.

Go back to other things you have written and write more about . . .

Can you check your journal for writing ideas?

Why don't you take a walk down the hall and write down all the things you can write about?

Can you check your favorite book and think of new ideas?

LIST #40 BOOKS TO HELP CHILDREN WITH WRITING

Milestones: Steckel, R., & Steckel, M. (2004). *The Milestone Project.* Berkeley, CA: Tricycle Press. The authors of this book traveled around the world to collect stories from people about important milestones in their lives. Some of the stories talk about birthdays, friends, haircuts, and responsibilities. Make a list of new words children can remember. Teachers can use this book to start their own milestone project by having students interview family members about their milestones. Place these stories in a class book.

Story Searching: Sortland, B. (2000). *The Story of the Search for the Story.* Minneapolis, MN: Carolrhoda Books. This is a wonderful story that will help children discover stories in all things. The illustrations are unique and will capture children's attention. Make a list of words that tell where stories were found. After reading this book, teachers can have children make a list of all the ways the character in the book discovered stories.

Book Lovers: Jeram, A. *I Love My Little Story Book.* London: Walker Books. Inspire children to love books by reading this special story. Invite students to share the books they love. Make a list of words that describe books they love, such as "funny," "exciting." Have them explain why they love each book. Teach children that they can refer to books they like when they write stories.

Asking Questions: Muth, J. J. (2002). *The Three Questions.* New York: Scholastic. To help children enrich their writing, use this book to teach them how to ask questions. Teachers can begin by reading until they come to the first question in the story. Next, have children think of a question they could write in their stories. Continue reading the story and encourage students to write questions when writing stories.

Resources

If you think about words as the building blocks for communication, it puts vocabulary learning in a different light.

~Judith A. Scott

Resource A

VOCABULARY SELF-ASSESSMENT

Teachers can use this vocabulary self-assessment to understand their beliefs about vocabulary instruction.

Directions: Read the following belief statements. Circle the response that reflects your beliefs about metacognition and reading comprehension.					
SD (strongly disagree) = 1, somewhat disagree = 2, neutral =3, somewhat agree = 4, SA (strongly agree) = 5					
Belief statements	*SD*				*SA*
Vocabulary increases reading comprehension significantly.	1	2	3	4	5
Vocabulary is easy for students to learn.	1	2	3	4	5
Using a dictionary at an early age is good teaching practice.	1	2	3	4	5
Children come to school with a repertoire of vocabulary knowledge.	1	2	3	4	5
Oral language development will enhance vocabulary knowledge.	1	2	3	4	5
To be a good writer, you need to have a strong vocabulary.	1	2	3	4	5
Different students have different self-regulation mechanisms they can use to remember words.	1	2	3	4	5
It is good to use word association teaching strategies to help students recall vocabulary meaning.	1	2	3	4	5
Monitoring is a comprehension strategy that can also be used when students read words they do not understand.	1	2	3	4	5
Frequent testing of vocabulary knowledge is important to vocabulary growth at an early age.	1	2	3	4	5

Resource B

READINGS ABOUT VOCABULARY

Blachowicz, C., & Fisher, P. (2002). *Teaching Vocabulary in All Classrooms* (2nd ed.). Columbus, OH: Merrill Prentice Hall.

A professional development tool for teachers who want to learn more about the theoretical perspectives related to teaching vocabulary. The authors focus on vocabulary theory, evaluate vocabulary instruction, and discover teaching vocabulary guidelines.

Beck, I. A., McKeown, M. G., & Kucan, L. (2002). *Bringing Words to Life: Robust Vocabulary Instruction.* New York: Guilford Press.

Teachers at all levels will benefit from the many valuable teaching strategies related to vocabulary. Teachers will also learn about tiered words, and how to increase students' vocabulary using tiered words. Children will enjoy learning new vocabulary games, and teachers and students both will learn to think differently about vocabulary instruction.

Fry, E. B., & Kress, J. E. (2006). *The Reading Teacher's Book of Lists* (5th ed.). San Francisco: Jossey-Bass.

This book expands on vocabulary development and offers teachers lists related to improving vocabulary instruction. The authors focus on explicit teaching of phonics, how to explore vocabulary word builders from Latin, French, Greek, and so forth, and how to expand spelling and comprehension knowledge.

Block, C., & Israel, S. (2004). The ABCs of performing highly effective think-alouds. *The Reading Teacher*, *58*(2), 154–167.

The authors describe the periods before, during, and after think-aloud strategies and provide lots of examples on how to effectively begin helping students develop metacognitive thinking.

Vukelich, C., & Christie, J. (2004). *Building a Foundation for Preschool Literacy: Effective Instruction for Children's Reading and Writing Development.* Newark, DE: International Reading Association.

Early Reading First initiatives sponsored by No Child Left Behind promote the development of phonological awareness, oral language skills, concepts of print, and the alphabetic principle. The book focuses on helping educators develop engaging curriculum that enhances all aspects of Early Reading First.

Morrow, L. M., & Gambrell, L. B. (2004). *Using Children's Literature in Preschool: Comprehending and Enjoying Books*. Newark, DE: International Reading Association.

Children's literature is a wonderful tool to enhance literacy instruction and to motivate children to read. This is a rich resource with ideas on children's literature that can be integrated into all aspects of the preschool curriculum.

Perfect, K. A. (1999). Rhyme and reason: Poetry for the heart and head. *The Reading Teacher*, 52, 728–737.

This article is for teachers who love poetry and realize it is a powerful tool in a literacy program. When children are introduced to poems in an environment that is accepting and safe, they will want to explore writing and become part of a shared community of poets.

Glazer, J. (1990). Poem picture books and their uses in the classroom. *The Reading Teacher*, 44(2), 102–109.

This article will help teachers learn more about poetry picture books.

Resource C

WEB SITES FOR TEACHING PHONICS AND LEARNING TO READ

www.nrrf.org

www.ciera.org

www.readingrecovery.org

www.eclkc.ohs.acf.hhs.gov/hslc

www.jstart.org

www.zoophonics.com

www.orton-gillingham.com/

www.letterland.com

www.benchmarkschool.com

www.projectread.com

Resource D

SCIENCE VOCABULARY AND WEB SITES TO INCREASE CRITICAL THINKING

This list is a valuable resource for exemplary teachers who want to build scientific vocabulary with their students, as well as enhance deeper thinking on the collection's theme.

Vital Vocabulary to Increase Thinking About Science Through Inquiry

analysis
analyze
assumption
capacity
communicate
confirm
consider
data
establish
evaluate
evidence
examine
explore
facts
figures
gather
indication
inquiry
investigate
observe
outcome
prove
query
question
research
results
revise
search
statistics
study
survey
verify

Teaching Goals to Develop Scientific Minds: Identify three goals or positive actions you would like to focus on related to inspiring students to think about science through inquiry, and to integrating science with literacy instruction.

Web Sites

The helpful Web site sponsored by the Smithsonian Museum (www.SmithsonianSource.org) offers many digitized resources that can be used for virtual history field trips. Another important and popular event, "Smithsonian Teacher Night," provides teachers with a multitude of helpful educational resources, books, author talks, and lesson plans. Registration for this event is required.

Students and adults of all ages will enjoy *Discover* magazine, which is filled with lots of articles related to the latest in scientific research, interviews with scientists, and critical thinking activities in math and science for children. The magazine always highlights issues, hot topics, and the latest science-related news stories. Visit www.discovermagazine.com to find helpful teacher resources, lesson plans, e-cards, and forums to enhance the magazine's contents.

The fictional book *Doctor Ecco's Cyberpuzzles* by Dennis Shasha can be used for a read-aloud in math or science. The book utilizes illustrations and puzzles with a story for the reader to solve.

Resource E

POETRY LEARNING CENTERS

Poetry provides a wonderful way to inspire vocabulary development. Many primary grade classrooms engage students by using learning centers. The following list of learning center ideas using the theme of poetry can be incorporated easily into the classroom. Teachers can modify the learning center ideas to fit other classroom themes, such as Native American. To integrate the learning centers with a Native American theme, locate poetry books with this theme.

Poetry Centers Focusing on Vocabulary Development

1. Poetry starters: Fill a box or file with phrases that students have cut out of magazines, famous quotes from poets, or adjectives that students have written down. Have students use the resources for brainstorming ideas for a poem.

2. Funny title time: Have students write down silly titles on index cards, or cut funny titles out of the newspaper. Use the title starters to help students get started on their poems.

3. Poetry picture ideas: Have a parent volunteer fill cereal boxes full of theme-related pictures. You can laminate the pictures so they will last longer. Students can use the pictures as a springboard for describing the characters or setting in a poem. The visual aid will help students be more descriptive in their writing.

4. Poetry picture book reviews: Place a collection of poetry books at a center with a box of index cards. Larger index cards are great because they provide more space and allow room for decorations or pictures. Have students read the picture books and write book reviews for their classmates. Classmates can add comments to the reviews.

5. Poets' corner: Locate a bulletin board in your room that students can access easily. Pin a variety of laminated words and phrases to the board so that they are easy to move around. Students can work in pairs and stand at this center to move the words around on the bulletin board to create a poem.

6. Junior poetic license: Encourage students to create a junior poetic license newspaper filled with poems they have written at the poetry centers. Use Microsoft Publisher to create the newspaper, or assist students in designing their own poetry paper.

7. Poets onstage: Have students read and act out poems that they have written or simply enjoy reading. Encourage the use of oral language and expression when reading poems. If the noise disrupts the other students, teach students how to use their whisper voices while onstage.

8. Getting to know poets: Provide a variety of stationery and writing materials and encourage students to write letters to famous and favorite poets. For an assignment, students can bring addresses to school with a stamped envelope, or have parents create a list of recommended poets from their state to write letters to.

Resource F

HOME–SCHOOL CONNECTIONS

Following is a list of vocabulary links where teachers can obtain vocabulary ideas to use in their classroom, or recommend for parents to use to make home–school connections. This list may also be included in a teacher or school newsletter.

Accelerated Reading Program—www.renlearn.com. Focuses on vocabulary integrated with literature.

Great Leaps Reading Program—www.greatleaps.com. Offers early literacy vocabulary skill development.

Letterland Computer Software—www.letterland.com. Uses word associations to teach vocabulary.

National Right to Read Foundation—www.nrrf.org. This is a national resource for teachers and parents. It offers many helpful links to other vocabulary development programs.

Read 180—www.scholastic.com. This is a visual software reading development program.

Zoo-Phonics—www.zoo-phonics.com. This site offers parents and teachers vocabulary and word learning activities and resources based on mnemonic skills research.

References

Beck, I. A., McKeown, M. G., & Kucan, L. (2002). *Bringing words to life: Robust vocabulary instruction.* New York: Guilford Press.

Biemiller, A., & Boote, C. (2006). An effective method for building meaning vocabulary in primary grades. *Journal of Educational Psychology, 98*(1), 44–62.

Blachowicz, C., & Fisher, P. (2002). *Teaching vocabulary in all classrooms* (2nd ed.). Columbus, OH: Merrill Prentice Hall.

Block, C. C., & Israel, S. E. (2004). The ABCs of performing highly effective think-alouds. *The Reading Teacher, 58*(2), 154–167.

Block, C. C., & Israel, S. E. (2005). *Reading first and beyond: A guidebook for teachers and literacy coaches.* San Francisco: Corwin Press.

Block, C. C., & Mangieri, J. N. (2003). *Exemplary literacy teachers: Promoting success for all children in grades K–5.* New York: Guilford Press.

Block, C. C., Oakar, M. M., & Hurt, N. (2002). The expertise of literacy teachers: A continuum from preschool to Grade 5. *Reading Research Quarterly, 37*(2), 178–206.

Clark, K. F. (2004). What to say besides sound it out. *The Reading Teacher, 57*, 440–449.

Cole, A. (2003). *Knee to knee, eye to eye: Circling in on comprehension.* Portsmouth, NH: Heinemann.

Duffy, G. G. (2003). *Explaining reading: A resource for teaching concepts, skills, and strategies.* New York: Guilford Press.

Ehri, L. C. (1995). Phases of development in learning to read. *Journal of Research in Reading, 18*, 116–125.

Frasier, D. (2000). *Miss Alaineus: A vocabulary disaster.* New York: Harcourt.

Fry, E. B. (2004). Phonics: A large phoneme-grapheme frequency count revisited. *Journal of Literacy Research, 36*(1), 85–98.

Fry, E. B., & Kress, J. E. (2006). *The reading teacher's book of lists* (5th ed.). San Francisco: Jossey-Bass.

Glazer, J. (1990). Poem picture books and their uses in the classroom. *The Reading Teacher, 44*(2), 102–109.

Green, V., & Enfield, M. L. (1974). *Guide to teaching phonics.* Bloomington, MN: Bloomington Public Schools, Independent School District No. 271.

Griffith, P. L., & Ruan, J. (2005). What is metacognition and what should be its role in literacy instruction? In S. E. Israel, C. C. Block, K. Bauserman, & K. Kinnucan-Welsch (Eds.), *Metacognition in literacy learning: Theory, assessment, instruction, and professional development* (pp. 3–18). Mahwah, NJ: Erlbaum.

Harris, T. L., & Hodges, R. E. (1995). *The literacy dictionary: The vocabulary of reading and writing.* Newark, DE: International Reading Association.

Howard, G. S. (Ed.). (2004). *For the love of teaching.* Notre Dame, IN: Academic Publications, Inc.

Israel, S. E. (2008). *Early reading first and beyond.* Thousand Oaks, CA: Corwin Press.

Israel, S. E., & Fry, E. B. (2005). *Vocabulary words primary grade students need to know.* Report for the National Reading Conference, San Antonio, TX.

Jobe, R., & Dayton-Sakari, M. (2002). *Info-kids: How to use nonfiction to turn reluctant readers into enthusiastic learners.* Portland, ME: Stenhouse.

Johnston, P. H. (2004). *Choice words: How our language affects children's learning.* Portland, ME: Stenhouse.

McIntyre, E., Kyle, D., & Moore, G. H. (2006). A primary grade teacher's guidance toward small-group dialogue. *Reading Research Quarterly, 41*, 1.

Morrow, L. M., & Gambrell, L. B. (2004). *Using children's literature in preschool: Comprehending and enjoying books.* Newark, DE: International Reading Association.

National Institute for Literacy. (2003). *Put reading first: The research building blocks for teaching children to read.* Center for the Improvement of Early Reading Achievement, NIL, Washington, DC. http://www.nifl.gov/partnershipforreading/publications/Cierra.pdf

National Institute of Child Health and Human Development. (2000). *Report of the National Reading Panel: Teaching children to read: Report of the subgroups* (00-4754). Washington, DC: U.S. Government Printing Office.

Perfect, K. A. (1999). Rhyme and reason: Poetry for the heart and head. *The Reading Teacher, 52*, 728–737.

Pressley, M. (2006). *Reading instruction that works: The case for balanced teaching* (3rd ed.). New York: Guilford Press.

Shasha, D. (2002). *Doctor Ecco's cyberpuzzles.* New York: W. W. Norton.

Sortland, B. (2000). *The story of the search for the story.* Minneapolis, MN: Carolrhoda Books.

Steckel, R., & Steckel, M. (2004). *The milestone project.* Berkeley, CA: Tricycle Press.

Vukelich, C., & Christie, J. (2004). *Building a foundation for preschool literacy: Effective instruction for children's reading and writing development.* Newark, DE: International Reading Association.

Vygotsky, L. (2000). *Thought and language.* Cambridge: MIT Press.

Wooden, J., & Jamison, S. (2005). *Wooden on leadership.* New York: McGraw-Hill.

Children's Book References

Blackaby, S. (2003). *A dog for you: Caring for your dog.* Minneapolis, MN: Picture Window Books.

Bray-Moffatt, N., & Handley, D. (2003). *Ballet school.* New York: DK Children.

Brennan-Nelson, D. (2004). *My teacher likes to say.* New York: Sleeping Bear Press.

Brown, M. W. (1977). *The important book.* New York: Harper Collins Publishers.

Brumbeau, J. (2000). *The quiltmaker's gift.* New York: Scholastic Press.

Carle, E. (1997). *Today is Monday.* New York: Scholastic.

Cronin, D. (2000). *Click, clack, moo: Cows that type.* New York: Simon & Schuster.

Cronin, D. (2003). *Diary of a worm.* New York: HarperCollins.

Curtis, J. L. (2002). *I'm gonna like me: Letting off a little self-esteem.* New York: HarperCollins.

Driscolli, M. (2003). *A child's introduction to poetry.* New York: Black Dog & Laventhal.

Edwards, J. A., & Hamilton, E. W. (2003). *Simeon's Gift.* New York: Harper Collins.

Fox, M. (1985). *Wilfrid Gordon McDonald Partridge.* New York: Kane/Miller.

Fox, M. (1997). *Whoever you are.* New York: Harcourt Brace.

Garland, M. (2005). *Miss Smith's incredible storybook.* New York: Puffin Books.

Grossman, V., & Long, S. (1991). *Ten little rabbits.* San Francisco: Chronicle Books, LLC.

Herrera, J. F. (2000). *The upside down boy.* New York: Children's Book Press.

Hoberman, M. (2004). *You read to me, I'll read to you: Very short fairy tales to read together.* New York: Scholastic.

Jeram, A. (2003). *I love my little story book.* London: Walker Books.

Jeunesse, G., & Delafosse, C. (2004). *Butterflies.* New York: Scholastic Books.

Lucas, D. (2003). *Halibut Jackson.* New York: Alfred A. Knopf.

Moulton, M. K. (2006). *Miss Sadie McGee who lived in a tree.* Nashville, TN: Ideals Children's Books.

Muth, J. J. (2002). *The three questions.* New York: Scholastic.

Nolen, J. (2006). *Plantzilla goes to camp.* New York: Simon & Schuster.

Reynolds, P. H. (2004). *Ish.* New York: Candlewick Press.

Scott, J. (2002). *Discovering dinosaurs.* Minneapolis, MN: Compass Point Books.

Seuss, Dr. (1963). *Dr. Seuss's ABC.* New York: Random House.

Seuss, Dr. (1990). *Oh, the places you'll go!* New York: Random House.

Shaw, M. D. (2002). *Ten amazing people and how they changed the world.* New York: Skylight Paths Publishing.

Slate, J. (1998). *Miss Bindergarten Celebrates the 100th Day of Kindergarten.* New York: Dutton Children's Books.

Stevens, J. (1995). *From pictures to words.* New York: Holiday House.

Wilkes, A. (1997). *Children's quick and easy cookbook.* New York: Dorling Kindersley Publishing.

Winters, K. (1996). *Did you see what I saw? Poems about school.* New York: Viking Press.

Wood, D. (2003). *Old Turtle and the broken truth.* New York: Scholastic Press.

Index

The Corwin Press logo—a raven striding across an open book—represents the union of courage and learning. Corwin Press is committed to improving education for all learners by publishing books and other professional development resources for those serving the field of PreK–12 education. By providing practical, hands-on materials, Corwin Press continues to carry out the promise of its motto: **"Helping Educators Do Their Work Better."**